Mastering Real Estate Math for Success

A Comprehensive Guide to Financial Calculations, Valuation, and Transactions in Real Estate

Ashton Kingsley

Copyright © 2024 by Ashton Kingsley - All rights reserved.

No portion of this book may be reproduced in any form without written permission from the publisher or author, except as permitted by U.S. copyright law.

Disclaimer

This publication is designed to provide accurate and authoritative information in regard to the subject matter covered. It is sold with the understanding that neither the author nor the publisher is engaged in rendering legal, investment, accounting or other professional services.

While the publisher and author have used their best efforts in preparing this book, they make no representations or warranties with respect to the accuracy or completeness of the contents of this book and specifically disclaim any implied warranties of merchantability or fitness for a particular purpose. No warranty may be created or extended by sales representatives or written sales materials. The advice and strategies contained herein may not be suitable for your situation. You should consult with a professional when appropriate. Neither the publisher nor the author shall be liable for any loss of profit or any other commercial damages, including but not limited to special, incidental, consequential, personal, or other damages.

CONTENTS

Introduction 6

Chapter 1: Basic Math Principles 8

   1.1 Fractions and T-Bar Method 8

   1.2 Conversions – Percentages, and Decimals 12

   1.3 Conversions & Equations 14

Chapter 2: Real Estate Calculations 17

   2.1 Basic Math Concepts 17

   2.2 Calculations for Transactions 25

   2.3 Proration Basics 27

   2.4 Commission and Commission Splits 28

   2.5 Seller's Proceeds of Sale 30

   2.6 Buyer Funds Needed at Closing 32

   2.7 Transfer Fee/Conveyance Tax/Revenue Stamps 33

Chapter 3: Land Measurement 36

   3.1 Metes-and-Bounds 36

   3.2 The Rectangular Government Survey System (RGSS) 38

   3.3 Lot-and-Block 43

   3.4 Points of Reference 45

   3.5 Measuring Structures (Homes and Buildings) 47

Chapter 4: Valuation and Market Analysis **49**

4.1 Appraisals 49

4.2 Estimating Value 51

4.3 Competitive/Comparative Market Analysis 67

Chapter 5: Financing **75**

5.1 Basic Concepts and Terminology 77

5.2 Mortgage 89

Chapter 6: Closing Statements **99**

6.1 Escrow or Closing; Tax Aspects of Transferring Title to Real Property 101

Conclusion **113**

INTRODUCTION

Welcome to "Mastering Real Estate Math for Success," an extensive manual created to close the knowledge gap between mathematical ideas and their real-world applications in the ever-changing real estate market. This book is designed for all real estate enthusiasts who want to understand the mathematics behind real estate transactions, whether they are seasoned professionals, aspiring agents, real estate students, or interested parties.

Why Use Math in Real Estate?

A strong quantitative knowledge is the cornerstone of every successful real estate deal. Math is a crucial skill in the real estate industry, used for everything from figuring out mortgage payments and comprehending interest rates to assessing investment properties and negotiating complicated closing documents. With the help of this book, you should be able to confidently and precisely manage the numerical components of real estate.

This manual provides a step-by-step overview of the many mathematical computations and ideas crucial to the real estate industry. To provide a strong foundation in basic arithmetic concepts, we start with the fundamentals and work up to more complicated real estate-specific computations and situations.

In Chapter I, you will learn the fundamentals of arithmetic, including fractions, conversions, and equations, which are essential for any real estate calculation.

Chapter II covers Real estate computations in feuding loan-to-value ratios and the finer points of transactional calculations.

Land measuring is covered in Chapter III and is essential for any property expert.

Chapter IV concentrates on valuation and market analysis to properly evaluate and contrast property values.

We dissect the intricacies of mortgages, interest, and other financial matters in Chapter V, which is devoted to financing—a vital component of real estate transactions.

Prorations and other closing charges are explained in Chapter VI, which addresses the closing statements, a topic that is often confusing.

In addition to explaining the ideas, each chapter includes activities and real-world examples to put away what you've learned. Infographics and other visual aids are used throughout to make more complicated computations easier to grasp.

This book provides a look into practical applications beyond theory. You may understand how mathematical concepts are used in real-world real estate situations by integrating case studies and real-world scenarios to give you a practical viewpoint.

More than simply a manual, it is a traveling companion on your real estate adventure. By the time you finish this book, you will have learned the fundamentals of mathematics and developed the self-assurance necessary to use these abilities successfully in your real estate endeavors.

Let's go off on this exploratory voyage where qualities meet numbers and computations result in success.

Chapter 1
Basic Math Principles

This chapter serves as an introduction to the basic mathematical concepts that are important in this area. This part makes sure your mathematical foundation is strong, from knowing how to deal with fractions to grasping the T-bar approach and converting between percentages, fractions, and decimals with confidence. These ideas aren't only theoretical; they're useful instruments that you'll use often in real estate deals. The abilities you acquire here will be your initial steps towards being numerically proficient in the ever-changing real estate industry, whether you're calculating loan-to-value ratios or interpreting intricate financial documents.

1.1 Fractions and T-Bar Method

In real estate, fractions play a crucial role and are widely used. Understanding fractions is crucial in various real estate transactions, from dividing property taxes to calculating commission splits and interest rates. This segment will thoroughly delve into real estate fractions, guaranteeing you have a strong understanding of these crucial mathematical concepts.

Exploring the concept of fractions

A fraction symbolizes a portion of a complete entity. The numerator is the top number, while the denominator is the bottom number. When dealing with real estate, fractions come into play to signify portions of an acre, ownership percentages, or splits of income and expenses.

Regarding property measurements, land areas are frequently described using fractions. For example, a land description could involve measurements such as 1/2 acre or 3/4 of a lot. Just as in financial situations, fractions play a crucial role. For instance, determining a commission split of one-third or realizing that a half-point in mortgage terms represents 0.5% of the loan amount.

Basic Operations with Fractions

Addition/Subtraction: To add or subtract fractions, make sure they have a common denominator. For example, to add ½ and ⅓, convert them to have the same denominator: ½ becomes 3/6, and ⅓ becomes 2/6, so 3/6 + 2/6 = 5/6.

Multiplication:

Multiply the numerators and denominators respectively. For instance, ½ x ¼ = 1/8.

Division: Invert the divisor and multiply. For example, ¾ ÷ 2/5 is the same as ¾ x 5/2 = 15/8.

Converting Fractions to Decimals and Percentages

Decimal: Divide the numerator by the denominator. For example, ¾ = 0.75.

Percentage: Convert the fraction to a decimal and then multiply by 100. So, ¾ = 0.75 x 100 = 75%.

Using Fractions in Ratios: A ratio can be expressed as a fraction. For instance, a ratio of 2:3 in real estate commissions can be written as 2/3.

The T-Bar Method

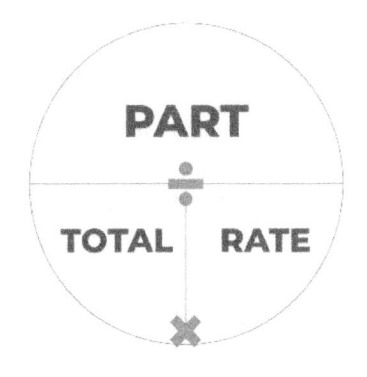

The T-Bar Method simplifies the comprehension and computation of fractions through visual aids. It's highly beneficial in the real estate industry for grasping relationships and proportions like those seen in loan-to-value ratios or property divisions. One way to approach this is by drawing a 'T,'

MASTERING REAL ESTATE MATH FOR SUCCESS

with the top part symbolizing the total or whole and the bottom part being split to display the fractional components.

Part = Total * Rate   Rate = Part : Total   Total = Part : Rate

Utilizing the T-Bar in Real Estate

For example, in a commission calculation, the total commission amount can be placed at the top of the T, and the bottom can be divided to represent the shares of the seller's agent, the buyer's agent, and any other parties involved. This approach provides a clear visual representation of fractions, simplifying the understanding of how the total commission is distributed.

A. Prorating Property Taxes

- **Scenario**: A property is sold, and property taxes need to be prorated between the seller and buyer. Assume annual taxes are $1,200, and the property is sold on July 1st.
- **Calculation**: The seller is responsible for ½ the year (6/12). So, the seller's share is $1,200 x 6/12 = $600.

Let's break down this scenario step by step to figure out the prorated property taxes for both the seller and the buyer.

1. **Total Annual Taxes**: The total amount of property taxes for the year is $1,200.
2. **Day of Sale**: The property is sold on July 1st. This is the 182nd day of the year in a non-leap year (since January has 31 days, February 28 days, March 31 days, April 30 days, May 31 days, and June 30 days).
3. **Dividing the Year**: The year can be divided into two parts: before and after the sale. We'll calculate how much of the $1,200 tax applies to each part of the year.
    - **Before July 1st (Seller's Responsibility)**: From January 1st to June 30th, which is 181 days.

- **After July 1st (Buyer's Responsibility)**: From July 1st to December 31st, which is 184 days in a non-leap year.

4. **Daily Tax Rate**: The daily tax rate is calculated by dividing the total annual taxes by the number of days in the year.

$$\text{Daily Tax Rate} = \frac{\text{Annual Taxes}}{\text{Days in Year}}$$

For a non-leap year, there are 365 days.

5. **Prorated Tax Amounts**:
   - **Seller's Prorated Tax**: Multiply the daily tax rate by 181 days.
   - **Buyer's Prorated Tax**: Multiply the daily tax rate by 184 days.

Let's calculate the exact prorated amounts for both the seller and the buyer.

Based on the calculations:

- The seller's prorated property tax amount is approximately $595.07.
- The buyer's prorated property tax amount is approximately $604.93.

These amounts add up to the total annual property tax of $1,200, allocated proportionally to the time each party owns the property during the year.

B. Commission Split Among Agents

- **Scenario**: Total commission on a sale is 6%, split between the listing and selling agents in a ratio of 2:1.
- **T-Bar Application**: Place 6% at the top of the T. Divide the bottom bar into three parts (representing the 2:1 ratio).
- **Calculation**: Listing agent gets 2 parts (4%) and selling agent gets 1 part (2%).

C. Calculating Loan Interest Rates

- **Scenario**: A $100,000 loan with an annual interest rate of 4.5%.
- **Fraction Conversion**: Convert 4.5% to a fraction (4.5/100) or a decimal (0.045).
- **Calculation**: Annual interest = $100,000 x 0.045 = $4,500.

D. Dividing Investment Property Income

- **Scenario**: An investment property generates $10,000 monthly income, divided among 3 investors in a ratio of 3:2:5.
- **T-Bar Application**: Place $10,000 at the top of the T. Divide the bottom into parts totaling 10 (3+2+5).
- **Calculation**: First investor gets $10,000 x 3/10 = $3,000, the second gets $2,000, and the third $5,000.

These examples demonstrate how fractions and the T-Bar Method are practical and vital tools in the realm of real estate. Mastery of these concepts not only aids in accurate calculations but also enhances understanding and decision-making in various real estate contexts.

1.2 Conversions – Percentages, and Decimals

Understanding and effectively using conversions between percentages and decimals is crucial in real estate, as these forms of representation are frequently used in various calculations, from determining commission rates to calculating loan-to-value ratios. Let's delve into these concepts and illustrate their application with practical real estate examples.

Conversions Between Percentages and Decimals

1. **From Percentage to Decimal**: Divide the percentage by 100. For example, 75% becomes 0.75 (75 ÷ 100).

2. **From Decimal to Percentage**: Multiply the decimal by 100. For example, 0.75 becomes 75% (0.75 x 100).

These conversions are fundamental in real estate because financial figures are often represented in both forms.

Practical Examples in Real Estate

1. **Commission Calculations**
   - **Scenario**: A real estate agent earns a 5% commission on the sale of a property.
   - **Conversion**: Convert 5% to a decimal for calculation (5% ÷ 100 = 0.05).
   - **Application**: If the property sells for $300,000, the commission is $300,000 x 0.05 = $15,000.

2. **Calculating Loan-to-Value (LTV) Ratios**
   - **Scenario**: A buyer purchases a home for $250,000 and applies for a loan of $200,000.
   - **Conversion**: To find the LTV, divide the loan amount by the property value and convert to a percentage.
   - **Application**: LTV = ($200,000 ÷ $250,000) x 100 = 0.8 x 100 = 80%.

3. **Determining Property Tax Rates**
   - **Scenario**: A property tax rate is 1.5% of the property value.
   - **Conversion**: Convert 1.5% to a decimal (1.5 ÷ 100 = 0.015) for calculation.
   - **Application**: For a property valued at $400,000, annual property tax is $400,000 x 0.015 = $6,000.

4. **Calculating Down Payments**
   - **Scenario**: A buyer needs to pay 20% down on a $500,000 house.

- **Conversion**: Convert 20% to a decimal (20 ÷ 100 = 0.20).
- **Application**: Down payment = $500,000 x 0.20 = $100,000.

5. **Interest Rate Calculations for Mortgages**
    - **Scenario**: A mortgage has an annual interest rate of 3.75%.
    - **Conversion**: Convert the interest rate to a decimal (3.75 ÷ 100 = 0.0375).
    - **Application**: For a $200,000 loan, the annual interest amount is $200,000 x 0.0375 = $7,500.

6. **Capitalization Rates in Investment Properties**
    - **Scenario**: An investor calculates a capitalization rate (cap rate) of 7% for a potential investment property.
    - **Conversion**: Convert 7% to a decimal (7 ÷ 100 = 0.07) for calculation.
    - **Application**: If the property generates an annual net operating income of $50,000, the property value estimated using cap rate is $50,000 ÷ 0.07 = approximately $714,286.

In conclusion, the ability to convert between percentages and decimals is a vital skill in real estate, playing a key role in a wide range of financial calculations. By mastering these conversions, real estate professionals can ensure accuracy in their financial assessments and decision-making processes.

1.3 Conversions & Equations

For precise computations in real estate, the ability to handle conversions and equations with precision is essential. These mathematical skills are essential for converting data, financial numbers, and measurements into information that can be put to use. Let's examine these ideas with an emphasis on how they may be used in real estate.

Real Estate Sector Conversions

1. **Area Conversions:** When measuring a property, it's customary to convert between several area units, such as square feet and acres.

As an example, a parcel of land has 43,560 square feet. Divide by 43,560 to convert to acres (one acre is equal to 43,560 square feet). There is one acre of land.

2. **Currency conversions:** It's crucial in international real estate deals since they may need the translation of pricing between several currencies.

Purchasing a home in Europe for €300,000 at a EUR/USD exchange rate of 1.2 is one example. €300,000 x 1.2 = $360,000 is the price in USD.

3. **Interest Rate Conversion:** Converting annual interest rates to monthly rates, or vice versa, is essential for calculating mortgage payments.

For instance, dividing a 4.5% annual interest rate by 12 yields a monthly rate. Rate each month is 4.5% ÷ 12 = 0.375%.

Equations in Real Estate

Loan-to-Value (LTV) Ratio: Real estate loan-to-value (LTV) ratio equations are as follows: LTV = (mortgage amount ÷ property value) x 100.

Example: LTV = ($200,000 ÷ $250,000) x 100 = 80% for a $200,000 loan on a $250,000 property.

Debt Service Coverage Ratio (DSCR):

DSCR = Net Operating Income ÷ Total Debt Service

An example of this would be a property with a $120,000 net operating income and $100,000 in yearly debt payments. $120,000 ÷ $100,000 = 1 is the DSCR.

Capitalization Rate (Cap Rate): The capitalization rate, or cap rate, is calculated as follows: 100 x (Net Operating Income ÷ Property Value).

As an example, consider a $700,000 property with a net operating income of $50,000. ($50,000 ÷ $700,000) x 100 = 7.14% is the cap rate.

Gross Rent Multiplier (GRM): A property's price times its gross annual rental income is the gross rent multiplier, or GRM.

An example would be a $500,000 home that brings in $50,000 a year in rental revenue. $500,000 ÷ $50,000 = 10 is the GRM.

Calculate Your Mortgage Payment: By using the formula:

$$PMT = P \times \frac{r(1+r)^n}{(1+r)^n - 1},$$

where P denotes principal, r represents monthly interest rate, and n is the number of payments, what may be achieved?

A $300,000 mortgage, for instance, with a 30-year term and an annual interest rate of 3.5%. The interest rate for the month is 0.035 ÷ 12 = 0.0029167 for ®. Thirty years x 12 months = 360 is the number of payments (n). Based on the calculation, PMT ≈ $1,347.

Real estate specialists must comprehend these conversions and computations. They are used in many different contexts, ranging from precisely marketing and appraising real estate to evaluating the financial sustainability of loans and investments.

Chapter 2
REAL ESTATE CALCULATIONS

2.1 Basic Math Concepts

A. Loan-to-Value Ratios

The Loan-to-Value (LTV) ratio is a critical financial concept in real estate, widely used by lenders to assess the risk of a mortgage loan. It represents the ratio of the loan amount to the appraised value or purchase price of a property, expressed as a percentage. Understanding and calculating the LTV ratio is essential for both lenders and borrowers in real estate transactions.

1. **Definition**: LTV ratio = (Amount of Loan ÷ Appraised Value or Purchase Price of Property) x 100.

2. **Significance**: It indicates the proportion of a property that is financed by a loan and the equity amount. A higher LTV ratio means more borrowing in relation to the property value, which is perceived as higher risk by lenders.

🔍 **Practical Examples in Real Estate**

1. **Purchasing a Home**

    - **Scenario**: A buyer wants to purchase a home priced at $500,000. They are approved for a mortgage loan of $400,000.
    - **LTV Calculation**: LTV = ($400,000 ÷ $500,000) x 100 = 80%.

- **Implications**: An LTV of 80% is often a cutoff point for avoiding private mortgage insurance (PMI). In this case, the buyer has a favorable LTV and may not require PMI.

2. **Refinancing a Mortgage**
    - **Scenario**: A homeowner seeks to refinance their home. The home is appraised at $300,000, and they have an outstanding mortgage balance of $200,000.
    - **LTV Calculation**: LTV = ($200,000 ÷ $300,000) x 100 = approximately 66.67%.
    - **Implications**: A lower LTV ratio is favorable in refinancing as it indicates more equity in the home and can result in better interest rates and loan terms.

3. **Evaluating a Loan Request**
    - **Scenario**: A real estate investor applies for a loan to buy an investment property valued at $750,000. The loan requested is $600,000.
    - **LTV Calculation**: LTV = ($600,000 ÷ $750,000) x 100 = 80%.
    - **Implications**: Lenders may scrutinize loans with higher LTV ratios more closely and might require additional guarantees or higher interest rates due to perceived risk.

4. **Home Equity Loan**
    - **Scenario**: A homeowner wants to take out a home equity loan. The current market value of the home is $400,000, and the remaining mortgage balance is $250,000.
    - **LTV Calculation for Equity Loan**: First, calculate the current LTV with the remaining mortgage, then determine the potential LTV post equity loan. Current LTV = ($250,000 ÷ $400,000) x 100 = 62.5%. If the homeowner wants

an equity loan of $50,000, the new loan amount will be $250,000 + $50,000 = $300,000, and the new LTV = ($300,000 ÷ $400,000) x 100 = 75%.

LTV ratios are indispensable in real estate finance. They are used by lenders to assess loan applications, set loan terms, and decide on the necessity of mortgage insurance. For borrowers, understanding the LTV ratio helps in evaluating the feasibility of a mortgage, understanding equity positions, and making informed decisions about property purchases or refinancing. A balanced LTV ratio is key to maintaining financial health and managing risk in real estate investments.

B. Discount Points

Discount points, often simply called "points" in the real estate and mortgage industries, are fees paid directly to the lender at closing in exchange for a reduced interest rate. This practice is also known as "buying down the rate." Understanding how discount points work is crucial for both buyers and those refinancing a mortgage, as it affects the overall cost of the loan.

1. **Definition**: One discount point typically costs 1% of the loan amount and usually lowers the loan's interest rate by a certain fixed percentage, which can vary by lender and market condition.

2. **Purpose**: Paying discount points is a form of prepaid interest. The borrower pays an upfront fee in exchange for a lower interest rate, which can result in lower monthly mortgage payments.

🔍 **Practical Examples in Real Estate**

1. **Buying a Home**
   - **Scenario**: A buyer is obtaining a mortgage for $300,000. The lender offers a rate of 4.5% with no points, or 4.25% for one discount point.
   - **Cost of Points**: 1 point = 1% of $300,000 = $3,000.
   - **Interest Rate Reduction**: Paying $3,000 upfront reduces the interest rate to 4.25%.

- **Decision Factor**: The buyer must decide if the upfront cost is worth the long-term savings in interest. This often depends on how long they plan to stay in the home.

2. **Refinancing a Mortgage**
    - **Scenario**: A homeowner is refinancing a $200,000 mortgage. The lender offers a rate of 3.8% with no points or 3.5% for two discount points.
    - **Cost of Points**: 2 points = 2% of $200,000 = $4,000.
    - **Interest Rate Reduction**: Paying $4,000 upfront lowers the rate to 3.5%.
    - **Break Even Analysis**: The homeowner needs to calculate how long it will take to recoup the $4,000 in exchange for lower monthly payments. If they plan to stay in the house long enough to pass the breakeven point, it might be a good deal.

3. **Investment Property**
    - **Scenario**: An investor is considering buying points for a loan on a rental property.
    - **Consideration**: The investor needs to weigh the cost of points against the potential long-term savings in interest. For rental properties, tax implications of buying points also play a role in the decision.

Discount points can significantly affect the total cost of a loan. The decision to buy points should be based on factors like how much cash the buyer has on hand, how long they plan to own the home, and the potential savings on interest payments over time. It's a financial strategy that can potentially save a considerable amount of money in interest but requires careful consideration and often a detailed break-even analysis to determine if it is a financially prudent decision.

C. Equity

Equity is a fundamental concept in real estate, representing the value that the property owner has built up in their property. It's the difference between the market value of the property and any outstanding debts (like a mortgage) that are owed on it. Understanding equity is crucial for homeowners, investors, and real estate professionals, as it impacts decisions related to selling, refinancing, or borrowing against a property.

1. **Basic Definition**: Equity = Market Value of Property - Outstanding Loan Balances.
2. **Building Equity**: Equity can increase through a combination of paying down mortgage debt and appreciation in the property's value. It can also be affected by changes in the market.

🔍 Practical Examples in Real Estate

1. **Home Purchase**
    - **Scenario**: A buyer purchases a home for $250,000 with a down payment of $50,000 and a mortgage of $200,000.
    - **Initial Equity**: Equity = $250,000 (home value) - $200,000 (mortgage) = $50,000.
    - **Over Time**: As the mortgage is paid down and if the home's value increases, equity grows.

2. **Refinancing**
    - **Scenario**: A homeowner wants to refinance their mortgage after several years.
    - **Equity Calculation**: If the home's market value has increased to $300,000 and the remaining mortgage balance is $150,000, then Equity = $300,000 - $150,000 = $150,000.
    - **Impact**: Higher equity can result in better refinancing terms or the ability to take out a home equity loan.

3. **Selling a Property**
    - **Scenario**: A homeowner sells their house.
    - **Equity Realization**: If they sell the house for $400,000 and the remaining mortgage balance is $100,000, then Equity = $400,000 - $100,000 = $300,000. This amount is the profit (minus selling expenses) the homeowner receives.

4. **Home Equity Line of Credit (HELOC)**
    - **Scenario**: A homeowner with substantial equity in their home decides to take out a HELOC.
    - **Equity Calculation and Loan Amount**: If the home is valued at $500,000 with a remaining mortgage of $200,000, the equity is $300,000. Depending on the lender, they might be able to borrow a significant portion of this equity.

5. **Negative Equity**
    - **Scenario**: A drop in the property's market value.
    - **Example**: If a homeowner owes $250,000 on their mortgage but due to market decline, the house is now worth $230,000, the homeowner has negative equity of $20,000. This situation is also known as being "underwater" on a mortgage.

Equity is a measure of financial health in real estate. For homeowners, it represents the portion of the property truly owned and not under any mortgage debt. It can be used to obtain additional financing or as a financial cushion in selling or refinancing decisions. For real estate investors, understanding and managing equity is crucial for investment strategies, especially when considering buying or selling properties, or leveraging equity for further investments. Accurate assessment of equity is key in making informed and strategic decisions in the real estate market.

D. Down Payment/Amount to be Financed

In real estate, the down payment and the amount to be financed are crucial concepts, especially in the context of purchasing property with a mortgage. The down payment is the initial upfront portion of the total purchase price that the buyer pays out of pocket. The amount to be financed, or the loan amount, is the remainder of the purchase price that is covered by a mortgage.

1. **Down Payment**: Typically expressed as a percentage of the purchase price. It affects the loan-to-value ratio, mortgage interest rates, and whether private mortgage insurance (PMI) is required.

2. **Amount to be Financed**: This is the total purchase price minus the down payment. It represents the principal amount of the mortgage loan.

Practical Examples in Real Estate

1. **Standard Home Purchase**
   - **Scenario**: Buying a home priced at $300,000.
   - **Down Payment**: If the buyer makes a 20% down payment, it would be 20% of $300,000 = $60,000.
   - **Amount to be Financed**: The remaining $300,000 - $60,000 = $240,000 will be the loan amount.

2. **Low Down Payment Programs**
   - **Scenario**: A first-time homebuyer opts for a loan program allowing a smaller down payment.
   - **Down Payment**: For a $200,000 house, a 3.5% down payment (common with FHA loans) would be $200,000 x 3.5% = $7,000.
   - **Amount to be Financed**: The loan amount would be $200,000 - $7,000 = $193,000.

3. **High-Cost Area Purchase**

    - **Scenario**: Purchasing in a market with high real estate prices.
    - **Down Payment**: Buying a $1,000,000 home with a 10% down payment means paying $100,000 upfront.
    - **Amount to be Financed**: The mortgage loan will be $1,000,000 - $100,000 = $900,000.

4. **Investment Property**

    - **Scenario**: An investor buying a rental property.
    - **Down Payment**: Investment properties often require higher down payments. For a $400,000 property, a 25% down payment would be $100,000.
    - **Amount to be Financed**: The loan amount will be $400,000 - $100,000 = $300,000.

5. **Refinancing with Equity**

    - **Scenario**: A homeowner refinancing their mortgage to tap into equity.
    - **Down Payment**: Not applicable in refinancing.
    - **Amount to be Financed**: If the home is worth $500,000 with a remaining mortgage of $300,000 and they take out a new loan for $400,000, the amount financed includes $100,000 cash-out from equity.

The down payment affects several aspects of a real estate transaction, including loan terms, interest rates, and the need for PMI. A larger down payment typically results in more favorable loan conditions but requires more upfront capital. Conversely, a smaller down payment makes home buying more accessible but often leads to higher monthly payments and additional costs like PMI. Understanding these dynamics is crucial for buyers to make informed financial decisions and for real estate professionals advising clients on property purchases.

2.2 Calculations for Transactions

a. Property Tax Calculations

Property taxes are a significant consideration in real estate, both for homeowners and investors. These taxes are levied by local governments and are based on the value of the property and the tax rate set by the jurisdiction. Understanding how to calculate property taxes is crucial for budgeting, assessing the affordability of a property, and for investment analysis.

Understanding Property Tax Calculations

1. **Assessed Value**: Property taxes are typically based on the assessed value of the property, which may differ from the market value. The assessment is conducted by the local tax assessor.

2. **Tax Rate**: The tax rate, often expressed as mills (where 1 mill equals 1/1000 of a dollar), is set by local governments. The rate can vary widely depending on the locality and the services provided by the municipality.

3. **Property Tax Formula**: Property Tax = Assessed Value x Tax Rate.

🔍 **Practical Examples in Real Estate**

1. **Primary Residence**
   - **Scenario**: A homeowner wants to calculate annual property taxes for budgeting.
   - **Calculation**: If their home is assessed at $200,000 and the local tax rate is 1.25%, the annual property tax is $200,000 x 1.25% = $2,500.

2. **Investment Property Analysis**
   - **Scenario**: An investor is considering purchasing a rental property and needs to calculate potential property taxes for ROI analysis.

- **Calculation**: For a property with an assessed value of $300,000 in an area with a tax rate of 2%, the annual property tax would be $300,000 x 2% = $6,000. This cost impacts the net operating income and thus the investment's attractiveness.

3. **New Home Purchase**
   - **Scenario**: A buyer is evaluating the affordability of a new home.
   - **Calculation**: If they are considering a home with an assessed value of $250,000 and the local tax rate is 1.5%, the annual property tax would be $250,000 x 1.5% = $3,750, which they need to factor into their annual housing expenses.

4. **Property Tax Appeal**
   - **Scenario**: A homeowner believes their home's assessed value is too high.
   - **Process**: They can appeal the assessment. If successful and the assessed value is lowered to $180,000 from $200,000, with a tax rate of 1.25%, the new tax would be $180,000 x 1.25% = $2,250, leading to savings.

5. **Comparing Properties in Different Locations**
   - **Scenario**: A homebuyer is deciding between properties in different tax jurisdictions.
   - **Calculation**: Comparing the property taxes in different areas is crucial. For instance, a $200,000 home at a 1.5% tax rate would have $3,000 in taxes, whereas the same value home at a 2% tax rate would have $4,000 in taxes, significantly impacting affordability.

Property taxes can affect the overall cost of owning a property and are a key factor in real estate investment analysis. For homeowners, these taxes are a major part of housing expenses. For investors, property taxes directly impact the net income from rental properties. Real estate professionals must be adept at calculating and explaining property taxes to clients to provide a comprehensive understanding of the financial aspects of property ownership or investment.

2.3 Proration Basics

The split or distribution of costs or profits between the buyer and seller depending on the percentage of time each party possesses the property during a billing period is known as proration in the real estate industry. This is sometimes required because, while certain costs, like homeowner association dues or property taxes, are paid annually, sales transactions might cause ownership of the property to change throughout the year.

🔍 Practical Example in Real Estate for prorations

Scenario:

- On July 1st, Alice sells Bob her home.
- The $2,400 annual property taxes are due on January 1st of each year.
- Alice has already made her annual property tax payment.

Goal: Compute Bob's property tax debt to Alice for the months while he has the property.

Resolution:

Determine the rate of daily property taxation: The yearly property tax is divided by the total number of days in a year.

$$Daily\ Tax\ Rate = \frac{Annual\ Tax}{365\ days}$$

$$Daily\ Tax\ Rate = \frac{\$2,400}{365} \approx \$6.58\ (rounded\ to\ two\ decimal\ places)$$

Ascertain how many days throughout the billing period each party is the owner of the property:

From January 1st to June 30th, or the first 181 days of the year, Alice is the owner of the property.

For the remaining 184 days of the year (July 1st to December 31st), Bob is the owner of the property.

Determine Bob's prorated property tax:

- ***Regarding Alice's share (181 days):***

$$Alice's\ Tax = Daily\ Tax\ Rate \times Days\ Alice\ Owns$$

$$Alice's\ Tax = \$6.58 \times 181 \approx \$1,191.98$$

- For Bob's portion (184 days):

$$Bob's\ Tax = Daily\ Tax\ Rate \times Days\ Bob\ Owns$$

$$Bob's\ Tax = \$6.58 \times 184 \approx \$1,212.72$$

4. **Total prorated property tax for Bob:**

$$Total\ Prorated\ Tax = Alice's\ Tax + Bob's\ Tax$$

$$Total\ Prorated\ Tax = \$1,191.98 + \$1,212.72 = \$2,404.70$$

Bob owes Alice $2,404.70 for the prorated amount of the year that he was the property owner.

Proration in real estate transactions ensures that costs are equitably split between the buyer and seller depending on the length of ownership throughout the billing period, as this example shows.

2.4 Commission and Commission Splits

The amount given to brokers or real estate agents for their assistance in arranging the sale or purchase of a property is referred to as a commission in the real estate industry. This fee is split between the buyer's agent and the listing agent, who represent the buyer and seller respectively. It is usually computed as a percentage of the selling price of the property. The division of the entire commission among these agents is referred to as a commission split.

🔍 Practical Example in Real Estate

For instance: Situation

- Alice is asking $300,000 for her home.

- Bob, a real estate agent, has been recruited by her to list her property. They decided on a six percent commission fee.

- John, a buyer's agent, has been retained by Sally, who is keen on purchasing Alice's home.

Goal:

- Determine the total commission that will be paid when Alice's home is sold.

- Ascertain the commission split between John, the buyer's agent, and Bob, the selling agent.

Resolution:

Determine the whole commission:

- ***Commission: 6% of the amount sold***

$$Total\ Commission = Sale\ Price \times Commission\ Rate$$

$$Total\ Commission = \$300,000 \times 0.06 = \$18,000$$

Establish the commission split:

- Usually, the buyer's agent and the selling agent divide the commission equally.

- In this instance, half of the commission will go to Bob and John.

Bob's (the listing agent) commission:

$$Bob's\ Commission = \frac{Total\ Commission}{2}$$

$$Bob's\ Commission = \frac{\$18,000}{2} = \$9,000$$

John's (the buyer's agent) commission:

$$John's\ Commission = \frac{Total\ Commission}{2}$$

$$John's\ Commission = \frac{\$18,000}{2} = \$9,000$$

In summary:

- $18,000 is the total commission that must be paid on Alice's home sale.
- The listing agent Bob will get nine thousand dollars.
- Nine thousand dollars will also go to John, the buyer's agent.

The operation of commission and commission splits in real estate transactions is shown by this example. The commission is paid to real estate agents in exchange for their services, and it is split between the buyer's agent and the listing agent in accordance with the conditions that have been negotiated between them.

2.5 Seller's Proceeds of Sale

In real estate, the seller's profits of sale are the funds left over after the costs and fees related to selling the property are subtracted. These charges usually consist of the remaining mortgage debt, closing costs, real estate agent commissions, and any other relevant fees. Subtracting these costs from the property's selling price yields the seller's profits of sale.

🔍 Practical Example in Real Estate

For instance: Situation

- Alice is asking $400,000 for her home.
- She owes $200,000 on her outstanding mortgage.
- Bob, Alice's real estate agent, has accepted a 6% commission payment from her.
- The total cost of closing includes $10,000 for title insurance, transfer taxes, and legal expenses.

Goal:

After subtracting the closing fees, real estate agent commission, and mortgage amount, figure out Alice's profits from the sale.

Resolution:

Determine the total cost:

- $200,000 is the mortgage balance.
- 6% of $400,000 is the real estate agent commission.
- Cost of Closing: $10,000

$$Total\ Expenses = Mortgage\ Balance + Commission + Closing\ Costs$$

$$Total\ Expenses = \$200,000 + (0.06 \times \$400,000) + \$10,000$$

$$Total\ Expenses = \$200,000 + \$24,000 + \$10,000 = \$234,000$$

Determine the seller's sales proceeds:

$$Seller's\ Proceeds = Sale\ Price - Total\ Expenses$$

$$Seller's\ Proceeds = \$400,000 - \$234,000 = \$166,000$$

In summary:

Alice's revenues of sale come to $166,000 after the real estate agent fee, closing charges, and outstanding mortgage debt are subtracted.

This is the amount of money Alice will get when her home is sold.

In this illustration, we can see how the different costs related to selling the property are deducted from the sale price to establish the seller's profits of sale. In order to calculate their net revenues from the sale of their property, sellers must have a thorough understanding of these expenses.

2.6 Buyer Funds Needed at Closing

In real estate, the buyer's funds needed at closing refers to the total amount of money that the buyer must have in order to finalize the acquisition of a property. These sums of money usually cover the down payment, closing charges, and any pre-paid fees related to the sale. All of these different costs must be added together in order to determine the buyer's closing costs.

🔍 **Practical Example in Real Estate**

For instance: Situation

- Bob is spending $300,000 on a home.
- He has secured a mortgage that requires a 20% down payment.
- Closing expenses total $10,000 and include attorney fees, title insurance, appraisal fees, and loan origination fees.
- For the first year, Bob must pay the whole $2,000. This includes both property taxes and homeowners insurance, as mandated by his lender.

Goal:

Determine the total amount of money Bob will need to bring to the closing table in order to close on the home.

Resolution:

- Determine the down payment amount.
- $300,000 was the sale price.
- Percentage of Down Payment: 20%

$$Down\ Payment = Sale\ Price \times Down\ Payment\ Percentage$$

$$Down\ Payment = \$300,000 \times 0.20 = \$60,000$$

Determine the whole cost of closing:

- Cost of Closing: $10,000

Determine the pre-paid costs:

- $2,000 in prepaid expenses

Determine the total amount of money required at closing:

$$Buyer's\ Funds\ Needed = Down\ Payment + Closing\ Costs + Prepaid\ Expenses$$

$$Buyer's\ Funds\ Needed = \$60,000 + \$10,000 + \$2,000 = \$72,000$$

2.7 Transfer Fee/Conveyance Tax/Revenue Stamps

The words "transfer fees," "conveyance taxes," and "revenue stamps" are used in real estate transactions to refer to levies or fees levied by municipal or state governments upon the transfer of property ownership from one party to another. These costs are normally paid at closing and are determined by the selling price or the property's assessed value.

🔍 Practical Example in Real Estate

For instance: Situation

- Bob is purchasing Alice's home for $400,000.
- One percent of the selling price is the transfer charge levied by the local government.
- A state conveyance tax equal to 0.5% of the selling price is also applicable.
- At the rate of $1 for every $500 of the selling price, revenue stamps are needed.

Goal:

Determine Bob's whole closing costs for transfer fees, conveyance tax, and revenue stamps.

Resolution:

Determine the transfer charge:

$$Transfer\ Fee = Sale\ Price \times Transfer\ Fee\ Rate$$

$$Transfer\ Fee = \$400,000 \times 0.01 = \$4,000$$

Determine the transfer tax:

$$Conveyance\ Tax = Sale\ Price \times Conveyance\ Tax\ Rate$$

$$Conveyance\ Tax = \$400,000 \times 0.005 = \$2,000$$

Determine how many revenue stamps are needed:

Ascertain how many $500 increments the selling price will have:

$$Number\ of\ Increments = \frac{Sale\ Price}{500}$$

$$Number\ of\ Increments = \frac{\$400,000}{500} = 800$$

Calculate the total number of revenue stamps required:

$$Total\ Revenue\ Stamps = Number\ of\ Increments \times \$1$$

$$Total\ Revenue\ Stamps = 800 \times \$1 = \$800$$

In summary:

- Bob will have to pay $4,000 in transfer costs in total at closing.

- Bob owes $2,000 in conveyance tax in total at closing.

- Bob has to pay $800 in total for revenue stamps at closing.

This example demonstrates how the selling price of the property is used to determine the amount of transfer fees, conveyance taxes, and revenue stamps. Since these fees are extra expenses related to changing ownership of the property, they should be carefully considered by both buyers and sellers in real estate transactions.

Chapter 3
LAND MEASUREMENT

3.1 Metes-and-Bounds

It can include:

- Specifying boundary lines and angles of a property.

- References to natural objects like rocks, trees, water (river or stream)

- References to artificial objects such as bridges

Metes and bounds is a legal documentation technique that is often used in property descriptions and real estate surveys to describe the boundaries of a plot of land. This approach defines the borders by locating the physical characteristics of the area, such as distances, monuments, and natural landmarks.

🔍 Practical Example in Real Estate

For instance: Situation

- Alice wants to sell Bob a chunk of the property that she owns.

- The metes-and-bounds approach is used to characterize the land parcel.

Goal:

- Recognize how the limits of the land are described using metes and bounds.
- Establish the precise limits of the area Alice wants to sell Bob.

Metes and Bounds Synopsis:

Starting Point (POB):

- This is where the land description begins.
- It might be an actual physical landmark, such a tree, stone, or crossroads.

Path and Length:

- The direction (course) and distance of each boundary line are used to characterize it.
- Degrees are used to indicate directions; they start in the north and go clockwise (e.g., N 45° E).
- Meters or feet are used to measure distances.

Landmarks and Monuments:

- Along the border lines, landmarks, both natural and man-made, serve as reference points.
- Trees, rocks, fences, and existing structures are a few examples.
- The explanation ought to conclude the loop by going back to the starting place.

Useful Illustration:

- Point of Beginning (POB): The northwest corner of the lot is marked with a stone marker.
- "Thereafter, N 45° E for 200 feet to a large oak tree" is the course and distance.
- "From there, travel 150 feet at S 60° E to a fence post."

- "After that, travel 100 feet at S 30° W to a small creek."
- "Thereafter, to the starting point, along the winding creek."
- Landmarks and Monuments: little brook, fence post, and oak tree.

The parcel of land is characterized using the metes-and-bounds approach by indicating precise directions, separations, and landmarks along the boundary lines. For legal and ownership reasons in real estate transactions, it is crucial to define property borders precisely and clearly, and this thorough explanation aids in achieving that goal.

3.2 The Rectangular Government Survey System (RGSS)

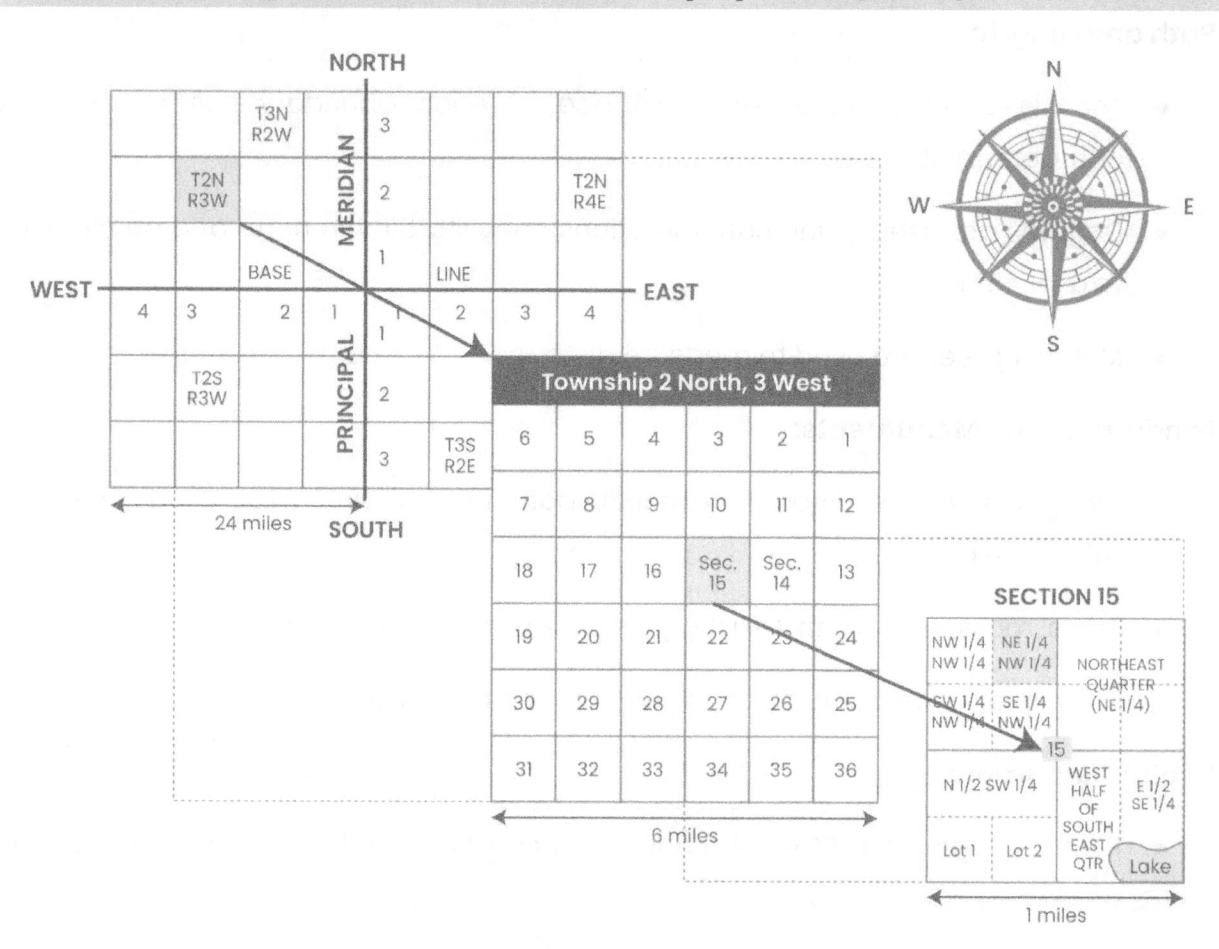

In the US, land parcels are divided and described using the Rectangular Government Survey System (RGSS), also called the Public Land Survey System (PLSS), which is based on a grid of fictitious lines. The United States government created this system to make it easier to administer and distribute public lands in an orderly manner.

Townships and sections are the rectangular divisions of land used in the RGSS. The 36 sections that make up each township are further divided, with each unit encompassing roughly one square mile (640 acres). Usually numbered 1 through 36, sections begin in the northeast corner of the township and move westward in a zigzag pattern known as the "government check."

🔍 Practical Example in Real Estate

For instance: Situation

Alice is interested in buying the land that the Rectangular Government Survey System (RGSS) describes.

Goal:

- Recognize the division and description of land parcels used by the RGSS.
- Find the exact place where Alice is interested in receiving the parcel.

Description of RGSS:

Range and Township:

- Townships and ranges make up the grid that organizes the land.
- A township is a square of land with 36 parts that is 6 miles by 6 miles in size.
- A column of townships stretching from north to south is called a range.

Sections:

- The 36 portions that make up each township are around one square mile in size (640 acres).
- Sections are numbered 1 through 36, with the first section being in the northeast corner of the township and moving in a zigzag pattern westward.

Sections that are Fractional:

Parts that are separated into fractional portions or situated on the fringe of a township may not be perfectly round. They may also cross over with a body of water.

Legal Synopsis:

A combination of township, range, section, and occasionally subdivision or lot numbers are used to describe a piece of land.

Useful Illustration:

- ***Township:*** Township 2 North, or T2N
- R3E stands for Range 3 East.

In this instance, the RGSS grid contains the piece of land identified as Township 2 North, Range 3 East, Section 12. Accurately identifying and finding land parcels requires an understanding of the RGSS, particularly in regions where it is in use, like many sections of the United States.

- RGSS Map Layout

Switch Mode

The Public Land Survey System (PLSS) is used in the United States to divide land parcels, and the RGSS (Rectangular Government Survey System) map style provides a visual depiction of this process. With this method, land is divided into a grid of townships, ranges, and sections, with a typical section covering 640 acres, or one square mile. It is necessary to comprehend the RGSS map structure in order to locate and describe land parcels inside the system with accuracy.

🔍 Practical Example in Real Estate

For instance: Situation

- Alice is interested in buying the acreage that the RGSS describes.

- She wants to find the parcel that interests her and learn how the RGSS map layout functions.

Goal:

- Recognize the arrangement of the RGSS map as it is shown visually.
- Find the exact place on the RGSS map where Alice is interested in buying a parcel.

The layout of the RGSS map:

Grid of Township and Range:

- Townships and ranges are arranged in a grid on the RGSS map.
- Townships are oriented north to south in rows.
- Columns of ranges are oriented from east to west.

Sections:

- Every township has thirty-six sections.
- Usually, sections are numbered consecutively from 1 to 36.
- Sections can be further separated into quarters, half, and occasionally smaller fractions.

Orientation in Direction:

- The RGSS map is arranged according to the cardinal directions: north, south, east, and west.
- Within a township, section numbers are assigned in a zigzag fashion, beginning at the northeast corner and moving westward.

Legal Synopsis:

- Township, range, and section numbers are used in conjunction to describe individual parcels of land.

- It may be necessary to supply additional lot or subdivision numbers for more accurate identification.

Useful Illustration:

- **Township:** Township 2 North, or T2N
- R3E stands for Range 3 East.

In this case, finding the matching township, range, and section on the RGSS map will allow you to locate the piece of land designated as Township 2 North, Range 3 East, Section 12. In order to facilitate land management, ownership, and real estate transactions, the Public Land Survey System's RGSS map style offers a methodical approach to see and navigate land parcels.

- Divisions of Sections

Sections of the Public Land Survey System (PLSS) and the Rectangular Government Survey System (RGSS) are frequently broken into smaller fractional parts to accommodate uneven boundaries or to make land ownership and management easier. Usually, fractional identifiers like halves, quarters, and smaller fractions are used to describe these divisions.

🔎 Practical Example in Real Estate

For instance: Situation

A portion of land in Township 3 North, Range 2 West that is identified as the northeast quarter of Section 8 belongs to Alice.

Goal:

- Recognize the fractional part division method for sections.
- Find the precise fractional portion of the section that belongs to Alice.

Sectional Divisions:

Split Half:

A segment can be split into two equal parts: the north (N½) and south (S½); the east (E½) and west (W½); quarters:

It is possible to further divide each half-section into quarters:

Northeastern (NE¼), northwest (NW¼), southeast (SE¼), and southwest (SW¼) quarters

Reduced Fractions:

- There are other fractional portions that can be made out of quarters, including the northeast quarter of the northeast quarter (NE¼ NE¼) and the southeast quarter of the northwest quarter (SE¼ NWµ).
- And so on, in accordance with the particular specifications of the land description.

Useful Illustration:

The northeast quarter (NE¼) of Section 8 is the designation given to Alice's property.

In summary, Alice's parcel in this example corresponds to one-fourth of the section, i.e., the northeast quarter. The limits of her land parcel inside the bigger section are more precisely defined and described thanks to this fractional designation. Accurately recognizing and defining land parcels within the RGSS or PLSS requires an understanding of the divisions of sections, particularly in real estate transactions and land management.

3.3 Lot-and-Block

In real estate transactions, the lot-and-block approach is employed to identify and characterize individual land lots. Under this technique, a block or subdivision's land parcels are subdivided into separate lots, each given a unique number. In urban and suburban settings where land units are smaller and more densely developed, lot-and-block descriptions are frequently utilized.

🔍 Practical Example in Real Estate

For instance: Situation

- One property that Alice is interested in buying is in a suburban area.
- A lot-and-block description of the property is given.

Goal:

- Recognize the operation of the lot-and-block scheme.
- Ascertain which particular block and lot of the property Alice is considering.

Lot-by-Block Overview:

Block:

- A subdivision's connected parcels are referred to as blocks.
- Every block is given a special name or identification.

Lot:

- A specific piece of land inside a block is called a lot.
- Within the block, a distinct number is given to each lot.

Division:

- A larger plot of land that has been split up into lots and blocks for construction is called a subdivision.
- Additional elements like streets, parks, or shared areas might be found in subdivisions.

Useful Illustration:

The Maplewood Subdivision's Lot 15 in Block A is the property in question that Alice is interested in.

In short, the lot number (Lot 15) of Alice's property in this instance is located within a certain block (Block A) of the Maplewood Subdivision. Property owners, real estate brokers, and governmental organizations find it simpler to handle and conduct real estate transactions in urban and suburban areas thanks to the lot-and-block system, which offers a practical and uniform method of characterizing and identifying land parcels inside subdivisions.

3.4 Points of Reference

Points of reference in real estate are certain geographic features or landmarks that are used to identify a property's location or limits. These points serve as a frame of reference for comprehending the property's geographic context and assist in determining the property's location in respect to its surroundings. Natural elements like rivers, mountains, and trees as well as man-made constructions like buildings, roads, and property signs can serve as points of reference.

🔍 **Practical Example in Real Estate**

For instance: Situation

- A piece of land in a rural location is being sold by Alice.
- The boundaries of the property are indicated by multiple points of reference in the description.

Goal:

- Recognize the usage of references in real estate descriptions.
- Find the precise references that were utilized to describe Alice's attribute.

Reference Points:

Natural Landmarks:

- Rivers: A property border may be defined as a river that it crosses or as one that runs parallel to.

- Hills or Mountains: Land might be defined as running up to the foot of a neighboring hill or mountain.
- Trees: Tree lines or individual trees can be used as reference points or boundary markers.

Artificial Structures:

- **Roads:** A property boundary may be determined by an intersection of surrounding roads or it may trace the route of a nearby road.
- **Buildings:** The positions of neighboring structures, like homes or barns, can be used to establish property lines.
- Physical markers erected along property lines to denote boundaries are called fences or property markers.

Examine Monuments:

- Land surveyors use physical markers known as survey monuments to precisely delineate property borders.
- Stone monuments, concrete markers, or metal stakes positioned at strategic locations along property lines are some examples of these monuments.

Useful Illustration:

According to the description, Alice's land is "bounded on the south by a line running due west from the oak tree at the corner of the property, on the east by the Johnson Farm, on the west by the Smith River, and on the north by Main Street."

The example's points of reference for Alice's property include the Smith River, man-made buildings like Main Street and Johnson Farm, and a particular tree—the oak tree—that acts as a border marker. These points of reference offer a precise and elucidating framework for comprehending the location and limits of the subject property.

3.5 Measuring Structures (Homes and Buildings)

Measuring real estate, especially homes and buildings, is crucial, especially when it comes to construction, evaluation, and property valuation. Precise measurements facilitate the assessment of a structure's dimensions, size, and arrangement—all of which are essential elements in evaluating its worth and appropriateness for different uses.

🔍 Practical Example in Real Estate

For instance: Situation

- Measuring a residential property for appraisal purposes is Alice's responsibility as a real estate appraiser.
- A single-family home with numerous rooms and features makes up the property.

Goal:

- Recognize the proper methods for measuring structures in real estate.
- Calculate Alice's property's overall square footage and the room sizes.

Assessing Organizations:

External Dimensions:

- First, determine the building's length, breadth, and height by measuring its exterior.
- Take measurements of the building's sides and note the measurements, being sure to take into consideration any projections or abnormalities.

Measurements inside the room:

- Determine the length, breadth, and height of every room's interior dimensions.
- Measure from wall to wall using a tape measure, taking into consideration any built-ins, closets, or alcoves.

- Take note of any height variances throughout the building and measure the ceilings.

Determine the Square Footage:

- A room's square footage can be determined by multiplying its length by its breadth.
- If a room has an irregular shape, split it up into smaller triangles and rectangles, figure out how big each one is, and add them all together.
- The overall square footage of the building can be calculated by adding the square footage of each room.

Useful Illustration:

- After taking measurements, Alice notes that the house is 40 feet long, 30 feet broad, and 20 feet high.
- She then determines the square footage by measuring the size of each room:
- Living Room: 300 square feet (20 feet by 15 feet).
- Kitchen: 180 square feet (15 feet by 12 feet).
- Bedroom 1: 120 square feet, measured 12 feet by 10 feet.
- Bedroom 2: 120 square feet, measured 12 feet by 10 feet.
- Bathroom: 48 square feet, measuring 8 by 6 feet.
- 300 + 180 + 120 + 120 + 48 = 768 square feet is the total square footage.

In this instance, Alice precisely calculates the total square footage of the residential property by measuring both its outside and interior dimensions. These measures are essential for figuring out how much the property is worth, evaluating whether or not it is suitable for renters or buyers, and enabling building or remodeling initiatives.

Chapter 4
Valuation and Market Analysis

4.1 Appraisals

An appraisal in real estate is a professional appraiser's assessment of a property's worth. For the purpose of establishing a property's fair market value, which is important to purchasers, sellers, lenders, and other parties involved in the transaction, appraisals are necessary in real estate transactions. A property's location, size, features, condition, and previous sales of similar homes in the neighborhood are just a few of the variables that go into an appraisal.

🔍 Practical Example in Real Estate

For instance: Situation

- Alice wants to know the current market worth of her home since she is selling it.
- She employs a qualified appraiser to evaluate her possessions.

Goal:

- Recognize how real estate evaluations are conducted.
- Based on the assessment, calculate Alice's house's approximate worth.

Evaluation Procedure:

Examining the Property:

- The property is thoroughly inspected by the appraiser, both inside and out.
- They evaluate the state, dimensions, design, and amenities of the property.

Examination of the Market:

- The appraiser investigates local comparable properties' (comps) most recent sales.
- They search for properties with features, location, size, and condition comparable to the subject property.

Analyzing Data:

- The information gathered from the inspection and market research is examined by the appraiser.
- They take into account things like additions, upgrades, and other special qualities that might have an impact on the property's worth.

Calculating Value:

- The appraiser establishes the property's estimated value based on their study.
- They take into account other pertinent information, adjustments for variances, and the sales prices of similar properties.

Report on Appraisal:

- The appraiser records their findings and conclusions in a thorough appraisal report that they generate.
- The estimated property worth, corroborating information, and justifications for the appraisal are all included in the report.

Useful Illustration:

After doing the evaluation, the appraiser concludes that, based on recent sales of nearby similar properties, Alice's property is worth $350,000.

Alice may utilize the appraisal's objective assessment of her property's worth to determine the price of her home for a sale or refinancing. Due to the fact that they provide lenders, purchasers, sellers, and other interested parties important information on the property's market worth, appraisals are essential to real estate transactions.

4.2 Estimating Value

A vital component of real estate, regardless of whether you're buying, selling, investing, or refinancing, is estimating the worth of a property. Comparative market analysis (CMA), the income technique, the cost approach, and the sales comparison approach are a few of the ways and methods used to estimate value. Depending on the kind of property and the availability of data, any approach could be more appropriate.

🔎 Practical Example in Real Estate

Let's examine this idea using a real-world illustration utilizing the sales comparison method:

For instance: Situation

- Prior to listing her property for sale, Alice would want to know how much it is worth.
- She chooses to compare her house to recently sold comparable properties in the neighborhood in order to apply the sales comparison technique.

Goal:

- Recognize how to use the sales comparison technique to assess the worth of a property.
- Based on recent comparable sales, determine Alice's house's approximate worth.

Approach to Sales Comparison:

Choose Properties That Are Comparable:

- Alice finds recently sold houses in her neighborhood that are comparable to her home in terms of characteristics, age, size, and condition.
- These homes should ideally be found in the same community or area.

To account for differences:

- Alice does a feature comparison between her home and similar ones.
- She adjusts for size, number of bedrooms and bathrooms, improvements, and amenities, among other variables between her house and the comparables.
- qualities that increase the worth of her property are given a positive adjustment, while qualities that decrease its value are given a negative adjustment.

Determine the Modified Sales Prices:

- Based on the discrepancies found, Alice modifies the similar properties' sales prices.
- To portray the comparables' values as if they were equal to her home, she adds or deducts the adjustment amounts from the sales prices of the comparables.

Calculate Value:

- By averaging the adjusted sales prices of similar homes, Alice determines the approximate worth of her home.
- As an alternative, she can make use of a weighted average determined by how relevant and similar each comparable attribute is.

Useful Illustration:

Three similar residences that have recently sold in Alice's neighborhood are identified:

- **Property A:** (same size, one less bathroom) sold for $350,000.
- **Property B:** Sold for $370,000; comparable characteristics, somewhat bigger
- **Property C:** Sold for $345,000; comparable size, less improvements

Following the necessary modifications, the revised sales prices are:

- **Property A:** $355,000

- **Property B:** $370,000
- **Property C:** $340,000

The average of the adjusted sales prices is the estimated worth of Alice's home, which is ($355,000 + $370,000 + $340,000) / 3 = $355,000.

In this instance, Alice used the sales comparison technique to estimate the worth of her home by contrasting it with recently sold similar houses in her neighborhood. She may price her home for sale or for other real estate objectives using this approach, which gives her a trustworthy estimate of the market value of her property.

1. **Economic Principles and Property Characteristics**

In real estate, the value, attractiveness, and investment potential of properties are largely determined by economic principles and property attributes. Making educated judgments in real estate transactions is made easier for buyers, sellers, investors, and other stakeholders when they are aware of certain traits and guiding principles. Property attributes like location, size, condition, and amenities impact the property's attractiveness and marketability, while economic concepts like supply and demand, utility, scarcity, and competition affect property prices.

🔎 **Practical Example in Real Estate**

For instance: Situation

- In a suburban neighborhood, Alice is thinking about buying a home.
- She is interested in learning how property attributes and economic concepts affect investment possibilities and property prices.

Goal:

- Recognize the fundamentals of economics and the features of real estate properties.
- Analyze the effects these variables have on the property Alice is thinking about, including its worth and attractiveness.

Principles of Economics:

- The relationship between supply and demand
- In a location where there is a limited supply of properties and a strong demand for them, property prices will probably rise.
- On the other hand, a property surplus compared to demand may result in a decrease in property prices.

Practicality:

Higher utility and value are associated with properties that offer desired characteristics and facilities, such as being close to parks, schools, and public transit.

Buyers find properties with practical design, good use of available space, and contemporary amenities more appealing.

Limited availability:

- Due to their scarcity, properties in locations with little land availability or distinctive features (such as waterfronts or historic structures) may fetch higher prices.
- Land use laws, zoning restrictions, and geographic limitations may also lead to scarcity.

Rivalry:

- Property prices are influenced by the degree of competition in the real estate market between buyers and sellers.
- Properties in marketplaces with intense competition and plenty of interested parties often sell for more money.

Features of the Property:

- One of the most important variables affecting property prices is location.

- Higher prices are paid for real estate in attractive neighborhoods with top-notch schools, low crime rates, and easy access to amenities.

Dimensions and Arrangement:

A property's size and arrangement, including the number of bedrooms, bathrooms, and square footage, affect its market value and buyer attractiveness.

State:

Good-looking houses with modern features and well-kept buildings usually fetch greater prices than bad-looking ones.

Facilities:

Features like outdoor living areas, swimming pools, and energy-efficient appliances may raise the attractiveness and value of a home.

Useful Illustration:

- Alice is thinking about buying a home in a suburban area with great parks, schools, and retail malls close by.
- She is drawn to a home with four bedrooms, three bathrooms, a large garden, and contemporary improvements.
- In the last several months, comparable residences in the neighborhood have sold for $400,000 to $450,000.

The example illustrates how economic concepts like supply and demand, utility, scarcity, and competitiveness affect the property Alice is thinking about in terms of its worth and attractiveness. A property's marketability and investment potential are influenced by factors including its location, size, condition, and amenities. Knowing these things enables Alice to decide on the purchase of the house with knowledge.

2. **Sales/Market Comparison Approach**

One of the most popular techniques for determining a property's real estate worth is the sales comparison approach, often referred to as the comparative market analysis or the market comparison approach. This method entails contrasting the subject property with comparables, also known as "comps," that have recently sold nearby. A real estate specialist or appraiser may determine the subject property's fair market value by examining the sales prices of similar properties and accounting for variations in features, size, condition, and other considerations.

🔍 Practical Example in Real Estate

For instance: Situation

- Alice wants to know the market worth of her home since she wants to sell it.
- She employs a real estate broker to use the Sales Comparison Approach in a Comparative Market Analysis (CMA).

Goal:

- Recognize how the Sales Comparison Approach determines the value of a property.
- Calculate Alice's home's estimated market worth using data from previous sales of similar homes.

Process of Sales Comparison Approach:

Choose Properties That Are Comparable:

- In terms of size, features, condition, and location, the real estate agent finds previously sold homes in Alice's neighborhood that are comparable to her own.
- These homes should ideally have sold within the last several months and be as near as feasible to the subject property.

Examine Similar Sales Data:

- The agent obtains data on the sales prices of similar houses as well as any pertinent specifics regarding their attributes, including the amount of square footage, lot size, number of bedrooms and bathrooms, and improvements.

- They also take into account variables like the date of the sale, the state of the market at the time of the transaction, and any unique circumstances related to the sale.

Make Modifications:

- To reflect the variations between the similar properties and the subject property, the agent modifies the sales prices of those properties.

- For instance, the realtor may take a certain amount off the sales price of a similar property to account for the fact that it has one more bedroom than Alice's home.

- Similarly, the realtor may raise the sales price of a similar home if it has more renovations or a bigger lot.

Calculate the Approximate Value:

- The realtor determines Alice's house's estimated market worth by adjusting the sales prices of similar properties.

- Usually, the average or median adjusted sales price of the similar properties serves as the basis for the estimated value.

Useful Illustration:

Three recently sold homes in Alice's neighborhood that are comparable to her home are pointed out by the agent:

- **Property A:** $420,000 was sold for.

- **Property B:** $410,000 was sold for

- **Property C:** $395,000. Sold

Following feature-based changes, the altered sales prices are as follows:

- **Property A:** $405,000
- $410,000 for Property B
- $390,000 is Property C.

The average of the adjusted sales prices ($405,000 + $410,000 + $390,000) / 3 = $401,667 is the estimated market worth of Alice's home.

In this case, Alice's house's market worth is estimated using the Sales Comparison Approach by contrasting it with recently sold similar homes in her neighborhood. Based on a property's attributes and the state of the market, this technique offers a trustworthy and impartial way to calculate a property's fair market value.

3. **Cost Approach**

One technique used in real estate evaluation is the Cost Approach, which determines a property's worth by subtracting depreciation from the cost of replacing or replicating its improvements. This method is especially helpful for valuing recently constructed or somewhat recently constructed properties when precise cost information is available or when comparable sales data is scarce.

🔍 **Practical Example in Real Estate**

For instance: Situation

- Alice is thinking about buying a brand-new office complex.
- She wants to use the Cost Approach to assess the property's worth.

Goal:

- Recognize the workings of the Cost Approach in real estate evaluation.
- Using this method, ascertain the office building's approximate worth.

Process of Cost Approach:

Calculate the Replacement Cost:

- Calculating the cost of replicating or replacing the property's upgrades is the first stage. This covers the price of labor, supplies, and overhead needed to create a structure that is comparable in terms of usability and purpose.

- In order to determine the current cost of constructing a comparable office building, Alice engages a contractor or construction expert to take into consideration several criteria such building size, design, quality of construction, and local construction expenses.

Depreciation factor:

- To account for any value loss resulting from physical degradation, functional obsolescence, or economic obsolescence, depreciation is then subtracted from the replacement cost.

- Physical depreciation is the term used to describe the aging, degradation, and damage that cause wear and tear on property over time.

- Useful obsolescence is the term used to describe flaws in a property's layout or design that make it less useful or desirable than similar recent constructions.

- Economic obsolescence is the term used to describe external variables that have an impact on the value of a property, such as shifts in the market, zoning laws, or neighborhood degradation.

Determine the Property's Value:

- Subtracting the total depreciation from the replacement cost yields the estimated worth of the property, which is the last step in the process.

- After depreciation is taken into account, the value that results is the property's estimated market worth based on the cost to replace or replicate it.

Useful Illustration:

- The contractor estimates that Alice will need to pay $1,500,000 to create an office block of a comparable design.

- The overall depreciation is $350,000 after accounting for depreciation variables such as physical depreciation from aging ($200,000), functional obsolescence from outmoded design features ($100,000), and economic obsolescence from shifting market circumstances ($50,000).

- Using the Cost Approach, the office building's estimated worth is $1,500,000 – $350,000 = $1,150,000.

In conclusion, the office building's worth is estimated using the Cost Approach in this case by deducting depreciation from the cost of replacing or replicating it. This methodology offers a valuable technique for property appraisal, particularly in situations when comparable sales data is scarce or for assessing recently started building projects.

4. Income Analysis Approach

The Income Approach is a real estate assessment technique used to determine the value of properties that generate income. It is also referred to as the Income Analysis Approach or the Income Capitalization Approach. When a property's revenue plays a substantial role in determining its value, such as in the case of investment, commercial, and rental properties, this method is often used to evaluate the asset. The Revenue Approach accounts for variables including rental revenue, operational costs, vacancy rates, and capitalization rates when determining the current value of the property's future income streams.

🔍 **Practical Example in Real Estate**

For instance: Situation

- As an investment property, Alice is considering buying an apartment complex.

- Her goal is to use the Income Approach to determine the apartment building's approximate worth.

Goal:

- Recognize the operation of the Income Approach in real estate evaluation.
- Using this method, ascertain the apartment building's approximate worth.

Process of Income Approach:

Calculate Your Potential Rental Income:

- Estimating the possible rental revenue the property may bring in is the first step.
- Based on the number of units in the building and the anticipated occupancy rates, Alice determines the possible rental revenue by looking up the rental rates for comparable flats in the neighborhood.

Subtract Collection and Vacancy Losses:

- Alice then accounts for possible collection losses and vacancies, which indicate the percentage of rental revenue that might be lost as a result of unpaid rent or vacancies.
- She makes an estimate of the vacancy and collection losses using industry standards or past data for the region.

Determine Your Effective Gross Income

- The total revenue the property generates after subtracting vacancy and collection losses is known as the effective gross income.
- By deducting the anticipated vacancy and collection losses from the possible rental revenue, Alice arrives at the effective gross income.

Calculate Your Operating Costs:

The running costs of owning and administering the apartment complex, such as property taxes, insurance, upkeep, utilities, property management fees, and reserves for upcoming repairs and replacements, are all estimated by Alice.

Subtract Operating Costs:

- Operating expenditures are deducted from effective gross revenue to arrive at net operating income (NOI).

- The NOI is the property's revenue before financing or debt servicing expenses are deducted.

Utilize the capitalization rate:

- The last stage is to calculate the value of the property by multiplying its NOI by a capitalization rate, or cap rate.

- The property's estimated rate of return, or yield on investment, based on market circumstances, risk considerations, and investor preferences, is expressed as the cap rate.

- To establish a suitable cap rate for the kind and location of the property, Alice looks into similar transactions and market data.

Determine the Value of a Property:

- By dividing the property's NOI by the cap rate, one may get the approximate worth of the apartment complex.

- The worth of the property as an income-producing asset is represented by this formula, which gives the present value of the property's future revenue streams.

Useful Illustration:

- According to Alice, the apartment block has a $300,000 annual rental revenue potential.

- The effective gross revenue is $285,00 after deducting a $15,000 collection loss and a 5% vacancy.

- According to Alice, the apartment building's annual running costs come to a total of $100,000.

- The formula for calculating net operating income (NOI) is $285,000 - $100,000 = $185,000.

- Alice concludes that an 8% cap rate is acceptable for the property.

- Using the Income Approach, the apartment building's estimated worth is $185,000 / 0.08 = $2,312,500.

In conclusion, the apartment building's prospective revenue and costs are used to determine its worth via the application of the revenue Approach. This strategy offers investors a useful way to assess income-producing assets and decide whether or not to pursue them as an investment.

5. Gross Rent Multipliers (GRM)

A straightforward technique used in real estate to determine the worth of an income-producing property based on its gross rental revenue is the gross rent multiplier, or GRM. By dividing the selling price of the property by its gross rental income, the GRM is computed. This method is often used to evaluate residential rental properties' values fast.

Practical Example in Real Estate

For instance: Situation

- Alice is looking to buy a modest apartment complex that contains four rental apartments.

- She wants to use the Gross Rent Multiplier approach to determine the property's worth.

Goal:

- Recognize the operation of the gross rent multiplier in real estate appraisal.
- Using this method, ascertain the apartment building's approximate worth.

Process of Gross Rent Multiplier:

Determine Your Gross Rental Income:

- The first step is to figure out the gross rental revenue of the property, which is the entire amount of rental money earned by each unit in the building before any costs are subtracted.
- To get the overall yearly rental revenue, Alice collects data on the rental rates for each unit and multiplies it by the total number of units.

Finding the Gross Rent Multiplier (GRM):

- By dividing the selling price of the property by its gross rental income, the GRM is computed.
- To calculate the GRM, Alice divides the apartment building's selling price by the entire yearly rental revenue.

Calculate the Property's Value:

After calculating the GRM, Alice may calculate the flat building's estimated worth by multiplying the total rental revenue by the GRM.

This computation gives the property's estimated worth based on its capacity to generate revenue.

Useful Illustration:

- Alice discovers a $500,000 listing for a tiny apartment block with four rental apartments.

- She finds that each property may rent for $1,000 a month after looking up local rental rates; this adds up to a total yearly rental revenue of $48,000 ($1,000 x 4 units x 12 months).

Alice calculates the Gross Rent Multiplier (GRM) using these numbers:

- Sale Price / Gross Rental Income equals GRAM.

- $1,500,000 / $48,000 ≈ 10.42 = GRM

Alice may determine the flat building's estimated worth using the GRM of 10.42:

- Value Estimated = Gross Rental Income × Ground Rent

- Value Approximation = $48,000 × 10.42 ≈ $500,160

In conclusion, Alice calculated the apartment building's worth in this instance using the gross rental revenue by using the Gross Rent Multiplier approach. The value of income-producing properties may be quickly and easily determined using GRM, but for a more thorough assessment, it's important to take into account other variables including running costs, vacancy rates, and property condition.

6. **Gross Income Multipliers (GIM)**

A straightforward technique used in real estate to determine the worth of an income-producing property based on its gross rental revenue is the gross rent multiplier, or GRM. By dividing the selling price of the property by its gross rental income, the GRM is computed. This method is often used to evaluate residential rental properties' values fast.

🔎 **Practical Example in Real Estate**

For instance: Situation

Alice is looking to buy a modest apartment complex that contains four rental apartments.

She wants to use the Gross Rent Multiplier approach to determine the property's worth.

Goal:

Recognize the operation of the gross rent multiplier in real estate appraisal.

Using this method, ascertain the apartment building's approximate worth.

Process of Gross Rent Multiplier:

Determine Your Gross Rental Income:

- The first step is to figure out the gross rental revenue of the property, which is the entire amount of rental money earned by each unit in the building before any costs are subtracted.

- To get the overall yearly rental revenue, Alice collects data on the rental rates for each unit and multiplies it by the total number of units.

Finding the Gross Rent Multiplier (GRM):

- By dividing the selling price of the property by its gross rental income, the GRM is computed.

- To calculate the GRM, Alice divides the apartment building's selling price by the entire yearly rental revenue.

Calculate the Property's Value:

- After calculating the GRM, Alice may calculate the flat building's estimated worth by multiplying the total rental revenue by the GRM.

- This computation gives the property's estimated worth based on its capacity to generate revenue.

Useful Illustration:

- Alice discovers a $500,000 listing for a tiny apartment block with four rental apartments.

- She finds that each property may rent for $1,000 a month after looking up local rental rates; this adds up to a total yearly rental revenue of $48,000 ($1,000 x 4 units x 12 months).

Alice calculates the Gross Rent Multiplier (GRM) using these numbers:

- Sale Price / Gross Rental Income equals GRAM.
- $1,500,000 / $48,000 ≈ 10.42 = GRM

Alice may determine the flat building's estimated worth using the GRM of 10.42:

- Value Estimated = Gross Rental Income × Ground Rent
- Value Approximation = $48,000 × 10.42 ≈ $500,160

In conclusion, Alice calculated the apartment building's worth in this instance using the gross rental revenue by using the Gross Rent Multiplier approach. The value of income-producing properties may be quickly and easily determined using GRM, but for a more thorough assessment, it's important to take into account other variables including running costs, vacancy rates, and property condition.

4.3 Competitive/Comparative Market Analysis

In real estate, a Competitive Market Analysis (CMA), often referred to as a Comparative Market Analysis, is a technique used to assess a property's worth by contrasting it with comparables—also referred to as "comps"—that have either recently sold or are now for sale. Real estate agents often use CMAs to assist sellers in setting a reasonable asking price for their property or to help purchasers evaluate the fair market value of a property they are considering buying.

🔍 Practical Example in Real Estate

For instance: Situation

- Alice, a homeowner, is thinking about selling her home.

- She wants to use a competitive market analysis to ascertain the property's fair market worth.

Goal:

- Recognize the operation of a competitive market analysis in real estate appraisal.
- Apply this method to get Alice's house's approximate worth.

CMA Procedure:

Choose Properties That Are Comparable:

- Choosing comparable properties that are similar to the subject property in terms of location, size, age, characteristics, and condition is the first stage in doing a comparative market analysis (CMA).
- In terms of these parameters, Alice's real estate agent finds recently sold homes in her neighborhood that are similar to her own.

Examine Similar Sales Data:

- The representative procures data on the features, attributes, and sales prices of homes that are similar.
- They take into account things like the square footage, lot size, number of bedrooms and bathrooms, condition, and any additions or modifications.

To account for differences:

- Subsequently, the agent modifies the similar properties' sales prices to reflect any discrepancies with the subject property.
- For instance, the realtor could increase the sales price of a similar property by a certain amount to represent the extra value if it has one more bedroom than Alice's home.

Calculate the Approximate Value:

- The realtor uses the modified sales prices of the similar properties to get Alice's house's estimated worth after making modifications.

- Based on current market activity, the estimated value offers a range or estimate of what buyers are prepared to pay for Alice's home.

Useful Illustration:

Three recently sold homes in Alice's neighborhood that are similar to her home are found by her real estate agent:

- **Property A:** $420,000 was sold for.

- **Property B:** $410,000 was sold for

- **Property C:** $395,000. Sold

Following feature-based changes, the altered sales prices are as follows:

- *Property A*: $405,000

- $410,000 for Property B

- $390,000 is Property C.

- Based on the adjusted sales prices of the similar properties, Alice's home is assessed to be worth $401,667.

In this instance, Alice's real estate agent determined the house's worth using a Competitive Market Analysis by contrasting it with previously sold homes in the neighborhood that were similar. With the help of this method, sellers may effectively ascertain the right listing price for their property depending on the demands of buyers and the state of the market.

1. **Selecting Comparables**

A critical stage in a number of real estate procedures, such as appraisals, market assessments, and listing price determination, is choosing comparables, also referred to as comparable properties or "comps." Properties that are comparable to the subject property include those that share its size, location, characteristics, condition, and other important details. Real estate experts can determine the subject property's worth, analyze market trends, and make well-informed judgements by contrasting it with previously sold or current listings of comparable properties.

🔍 Practical Example in Real Estate

For instance: Situation

- Bob, Alice's customer, is a real estate agent, and she is assisting him in deciding on the listing price for his home.
- In order to do a Comparative Market Analysis (CMA) and determine Bob's property's worth, she must choose comparables.

Goal:

- Recognize how to choose comparables in the real estate market.
- Choose comparables that are appropriate for Bob's home based on predetermined standards.

Process of Choosing Comparables:

Determine the Criteria:

- Alice starts out by outlining the critical selection criteria for comparables. Location, size, age, characteristics, condition, and recent sales activity are typical examples of these factors.
- For instance, Bob lives in a suburban neighborhood in a single-family home with three bedrooms and two bathrooms.

Look up Comparable Properties:

- Alice looks for recently sold homes and current listings in Bob's neighborhood that fit the specified criteria using multiple listing services (MLS), real estate databases, and other resources.

- In order to make sure the data she collects on houses that have sold in the last six months accurately reflects the state of the market.

Reduced Selection:

- Alice creates a list of possible comparables and then selects them by gauging how closely they resemble the subject property.

- She takes into account things like how close the subject property is, how similar the size and layout are, what features and facilities are similar, and how similar the condition is.

Check for Accurate Data:

- For every similar property, Alice confirms that the information about sales prices, features, and transactional details is accurate.

- She makes sure the data for the Comparative Market Analysis is accurate and up to date.

Make Modifications:

- Alice modifies the comparables' statistics to reflect any variations that may exist between the subject home and the comparables, such as more bedrooms, a bigger lot, or more recent renovations.

- The sales prices of the comparables are usually adjusted to represent their worth as if they were the same as the subject property.

Useful Illustration:

Alice finds three recently sold homes in Bob's neighborhood that almost meet the requirements for comparables after doing some research:

- **Property A:** $420,000 was sold for.
- **Property B:** $410,000 was sold for
- **Property C:** $395,000. Sold

The square footage, lot size, number of bedrooms and bathrooms, and general condition of these homes are all comparable.

In summary, Alice chose comparables for Bob's home in this instance by locating homes that substantially matched the requirements and features of the subject property. Real estate experts may provide their clients accurate appraisals, market insights, and suggestions by carefully choosing and evaluating comparables.

2. **Adjusting Comparables**

Making modifications to comparable properties, or adjusting comparables, is an essential stage in real estate valuation procedures including property assessments and comparative market analyses (CMAs). Upon comparing a subject property with similar properties (comps), disparities in characteristics, size, condition, or other variables that may impact their value are often observed. To account for these variations and make comparable sales prices more similar to the subject property, adjustments are made to the comparables' sales prices.

🔎 **Practical Example in Real Estate**

For instance: Situation

For her client Bob, a real estate agent, Alice is doing a Comparative Market Analysis (CMA) in order to help him sell his home.

She has to alter the sales prices of the three similar houses she found in Bob's neighborhood to reflect the variances from Bob's home.

Goal:

- Recognize how comparables are adjusted in real estate appraisal.
- Ascertain the necessary modifications to enhance the comparables' similarity to the property under consideration.

Modifying the Comparables Procedure:

Determine Disparities:

- Alice starts out by noting the distinctions between the subject property and the comparables. A few examples of these variations may include size, location, amenities, condition, and recent renovations.
- For example, the adjustment must take into consideration the fact that Bob's home has one more bedroom than a similar property.

Calculate the Amounts of Adjustment:

- Alice then calculates the adjustment amounts for each discrepancy that has been found. Depending on whether the change increases or decreases the value of the similar property, these modifications may be positive or negative.
- For instance, if the subject property has a bigger lot than a similar property, Alice can increase the comparable property's sales price by a certain amount to account for the larger lot's increased worth.

Make the necessary adjustments:

- In order to make the comparable sales prices more similar to the subject property, Alice adds the adjustment amounts to those sales prices.
- To account for qualities or amenities that the subject property possesses but the comparables do not, positive adjustments are made to the sales prices of comparables.

- To account for qualities or facilities that the subject property lacks but the comparables have, negative adjustments are deducted from the sales prices of the comparables.

Examine comparables again:

- Alice revises the comparables after making the necessary changes to make sure they are now more like the subject property.

- She confirms that, when compared to the subject property, the adjusted sales prices fairly represent the worth of the comparables.

Useful Illustration:

- Alice found a similar home that sold for $400,000, except Bob's home had one more bedroom.

- It is her determination that Bob's home is worth $20,000 more because of the extra bedroom.

- In order to account for the extra bedroom, Alice adds $20,000 to the sales price of the similar, making it $420,000.

In summary, Alice modified comparables in this instance to take into consideration variations from the subject property in a comparative market analysis. Real estate agents may assist their customers make well-informed choices about purchasing or selling real estate by providing them with more accurate appraisals and market insights via the meticulous identification and application of adjustments. By adjusting comparables, one may make sure that comparable sales prices accurately represent their worth in relation to the subject property.

Chapter 5
Financing

In the context of real estate, financing describes the procedures and systems used to raise money for investing in or buying real estate. Both people and organizations have access to a variety of funding choices, from conventional mortgages to unconventional finance arrangements. For all parties involved in a transaction—buyers, sellers, investors, and real estate professionals—understanding finance is essential.

🔍 Practical Example in Real Estate

For instance: Situation

- Alice's dream home would be a condominium that she would own.
- To find the best method to finance her purchase, she has to investigate her possibilities for financing.

Goal:

- Recognize the several real estate finance choices accessible.
- Ascertain which financing option is best for Alice's condo purchase.

Options for Financing:

Traditional Mortgage:

Alice is able to apply to a bank or other financial institution for a standard mortgage. Usually, a traditional mortgage requires her to pay back the loan plus interest over a certain period of time (such as 15 or 30 years) plus a down payment that is generally 20% of the purchase price.

Government-Supported Credit:

As an alternative, Alice could be eligible for government-guaranteed loans from the Department of Veterans Affairs (VA) or the Federal Housing Administration (FHA). These loans are appropriate for first-time homeowners or those with limited funds since they often feature more flexible qualifying requirements and lower down payment requirements.

Financed by the Seller:

Alice may be able to work out a deal with the seller to finance all or part of the purchase price in certain circumstances. If Alice finds it difficult to get conventional finance or if the seller provides advantageous conditions, this arrangement may be advantageous.

Hard money loans or private lenders:

Alice might look into hard money loans or private lenders for funding possibilities. These loans usually have longer terms and higher interest rates, but they may be more accessible for those with bad credit or unusual financial circumstances.

Innovative Finance Solutions:

Real estate finance comes in many unique forms, such as seller carry-back financing, wrap-around mortgages, and lease-to-own arrangements. These agreements include special clauses and frameworks designed to meet the demands of both buyers and sellers.

Useful Illustration:

- Alice chooses to apply to her bank for a traditional mortgage after considering her choices. She intends to repay the loan over a 30-year period and has saved enough for a 20% down payment.

- After getting in touch with her bank, Alice fills out the mortgage application and provides proof of her assets, income, and credit history.

- Alice completes the mortgage agreement with her bank, which includes the loan amount, interest rate, conditions of repayment, and other pertinent information, after being approved.

Alice considered a variety of financing solutions before deciding to finance the purchase of a condominium using a traditional mortgage. Comprehending the many financing alternatives in real estate enables purchasers such as Alice to make well-informed choices and get the essential capital to fulfill their aspirations of becoming property owners.

5.1 Basic Concepts and Terminology

Fundamental ideas and words that are necessary to comprehend the real estate market, transactions, and property assessment are included in the basic concepts and vocabulary of the field. Everyone engaged in real estate, including buyers, sellers, investors, brokers, and appraisers, has to understand these ideas.

🔍 Practical Example in Real Estate

For instance: Situation

Bob is interested in buying a house for the first time. He needs assistance to grasp the fundamentals as he is not acquainted with the language or ideas around real estate.

Goal:

Using real-world examples, introduce Bob to important real estate terms and ideas.

Fundamental Ideas and Terms:

Types of Properties:

Residential: Real estate that is intended for habitation, including apartments, townhomes, condos, and single-family homes.

Commercial properties include office buildings, retail stores, industrial warehouses, and hotels that are utilized for commercial or investment reasons.

Land: Undeveloped sections of land that are good for investments or construction.

Value in the Market:

- The price that a property would normally sell for in a competitive market, taking into account demand, size, location, and other variables.

- For instance, a home's market value is $300,000 based on recent sales of nearby homes that are comparable to it.

Evaluation:

A fair assessment of a property's worth made by a certified appraiser using a variety of techniques, such as cost analysis, income approach, and comparable transactions.

Example: In order to make sure the house's valuation satisfies the loan conditions, Bob's lender demands an assessment of the property before approving a mortgage.

Comparing Listing and Selling Prices:

- **Listing Price:** The amount that the seller or listing agency lists a property for sale for.

- **Selling Price:** The real amount that is paid to finalize the deal and sell the property.

- **Example:** Bob pays $310,000 for the home following talks, even though the seller had listed it for $320,000.

- **Requirement for Down Payment:**

- The first down payment paid by the buyer towards the property's purchase price; this amount is usually stated as a percentage of the overall cost of the acquisition.

- For instance, Bob consents to put down $62,000, or 20% of the $310,000 purchase price, on a home.

Mortgage:

- A loan made possible by a lender (bank, mortgage business, etc.) that is used to fund the acquisition of real estate and is secured by the real estate.

- Example: Bob finances the purchase of his home with a 30-year fixed-rate mortgage from his bank.

Closing Expenses:

costs spent by purchasers and sellers in the course of the real estate transaction, such as taxes, title insurance, escrow fees, appraisal fees, and loan origination fees.

For instance: Closing expenses, which include pre-paid property taxes, title insurance, and lender fees, come to around $8,000.

In conclusion, Bob gains knowledge of fundamental real estate terms and ideas via this example, including kinds of properties, market value, appraisal, listing price, selling price, down payment, mortgage, and closing fees. Bob may make wise selections throughout the home-buying process by being aware of these basic ideas, which also help him be ready for the process.

Points:

1. **Loan-to-Value (LTV)**

A key idea in real estate finance is the loan-to-value (LTV) ratio, which shows how much of a loan is compared to the purchase price or property's assessed worth. LTV is the greatest amount that a lender will lend to a borrower and is used by lenders to evaluate the risk involved with a mortgage loan. When looking for financing to buy or refinance real estate, borrowers must understand the Loan-to-Value ratio.

Let's examine this idea using a real-world example:

For instance: Situation

- Bob would want to spend $250,000 on a home.

- He wants to know his loan-to-value ratio since he intends to get a mortgage to fund the purchase.

Goal:

- Recognize the meaning of the Loan-to-Value (LTV) ratio in financing for real estate.
- Determine Bob's loan-to-value ratio by multiplying the mortgage amount by the house's purchase price.

Calculating Loan-to-Value:

Calculate the Loan Amount:

- Finding out how much of a mortgage loan Bob will need to fund the purchase of the property is the first step.
- Assume Bob intends to pay 20% of the purchase price up front and get a mortgage to cover the other 80%.

Determine the Loan Amount:

- Bob has put down $50,000, or 20% of $250,000. Thus, the $250,000 (purchase price) - $50,000 (down payment) equals the $200,000 loan amount that he needs.
- Determine the LTV Ratio.
- The Loan-to-Value (LTV) ratio is computed as a percentage by dividing the loan amount by the property's appraised value or purchase price.
- In Bob's instance, the home was purchased for $250,000, and the loan amount is $200,000.
- LTV Ratio is calculated as follows: ($200,000 / $250,000) × 100% = 0.80 × 100% = 80%.

Useful Illustration:

For the acquisition of the home, Bob's loan-to-value (LTV) ratio is 80%. This indicates that he is making a 20% down payment and that the mortgage amount he is requesting is equivalent to 80% of the property's buying price.

In summary, Bob used the purchase price of the home and the required mortgage amount to determine his loan-to-value (LTV) ratio after learning about the idea in real estate finance. Lenders use the loan-to-value ratio (LTV ratio) to determine loan eligibility, interest rates, and mortgage insurance obligations. Bob and other borrowers may evaluate their financing alternatives and make well-informed decisions about buying real estate by having a solid understanding of LTV.

2. Private Mortgage Insurance (PMI)

An insurance policy known as private mortgage insurance (PMI) protects lenders against financial loss in the event that a borrower defaults on a mortgage loan with a down payment of less than 20% of the cost of the property. PMI makes homeownership more accessible to those who may not have enough resources for a bigger down payment by enabling borrowers to receive financing for a home purchase with a lesser down payment. The borrower's monthly mortgage payments usually include PMI premiums until the loan-to-value (LTV) ratio falls below 80%.

🔍 Practical Example in Real Estate

For instance: Situation

- Alice has saved just enough for a 10% down payment on the $300,000 home she wants to buy.

- She wants to get a mortgage, but she needs to know how her monthly payments would be affected by Private Mortgage Insurance (PMI).

Goal:

- Recognize the meaning of Private Mortgage Insurance (PMI) as it relates to financing for real estate.

MASTERING REAL ESTATE MATH FOR SUCCESS

- Determine Alice's monthly mortgage payment and the effect of her PMI charge.

PMI Estimation:

Calculate the Loan Amount:

Alice is contributing $30,000. This is 10% of the $300,000 buying price. As a result, the $300,000 purchase price less the $30,000 down payment equals the $270,000 loan amount that she needs.

Loan-to-Value (LTV) Ratio calculation:

- The loan amount is divided by the property's purchase price to get Alice's Loan-to-Value (LTV) ratio, which is then expressed as a percentage.
- LTV Ratio is calculated as follows: ($270,000 / $300,000) times 100% of the loan amount. 90% × 100% = 0.90 × 100%

Calculate the PMI Rate:

The down payment size, loan length, and borrower's credit score are among the variables that affect PMI rates. Assume that Alice's yearly PMI rate is 0.5% of the loan amount.

Compute the PMI Premium:

- The monthly premium for Alice's PMI is computed as a percentage of the loan amount and divided by 12.
- (Loan Amount × PMI Rate) / 12 months = ($270,000 × 0.005) / 12 = $1,125 / 12 = $93.75 monthly for PMI Premium.

Useful Illustration:

- Until Alice's Loan-to-Value (LTV) ratio falls below 80%, her monthly mortgage payments will be increased by the roughly $93.75 monthly PMI charge.
- Alice may ask for PMI to be canceled whenever her loan-to-value ratio (LTV) hits 80%, either by paying off the loan debt or by the property's value increasing.

In conclusion, Alice gained knowledge about Private Mortgage Insurance (PMI) in this case and how it affected her monthly mortgage payments when she bought a house with a less than 20% down payment. It is easier for borrowers like Alice to evaluate the costs of homeownership and choose their financing choices when they are aware of PMI.

3. Interest

The cost of borrowing money for a mortgage loan or the return received on investment properties or real estate-related ventures are referred to as "interest" in the context of real estate. In exchange for the lender's use of their money, borrowers who get mortgages pay interest to the lender. Interest makes up a significant portion of the entire cost of homeownership and is often stated as an annual percentage rate (APR).

🔎 **Practical Example in Real Estate**

For instance: Situation

- Bob intends to apply for a mortgage in order to fund the $250,000 cost of the home he is buying.
- He's curious about interest rates and how they affect his monthly mortgage payments.

Goal:

- Recognize the meaning of interest in finance for real estate.
- Compute Bob's monthly mortgage payment and the total amount of interest he will pay on the loan.
- Interest Calculation

Calculate the Loan Amount:

Assuming Bob puts $50,000 down as part of the 20% down payment on the $250,000 property, he will have a $200,000 mortgage loan balance.

Calculate the interest rate:

Bob receives an offer from his lender for a 4.5% annual interest rate fixed-rate mortgage.

Compute Interest Payment Each Month:

- Bob multiplies the monthly interest payment by the outstanding loan sum after dividing the yearly interest rate by 12 to get the monthly interest payment.

- Interest Payment per Month = (Annual Interest Rate / 12) × Loan Balance Remaining = (0.045 / 12) × $200,000 ≈ $750

Useful Illustration:

With a 4.5% interest rate on his $200,000 home loan, Bob pays around $750 in interest each month. This indicates that $750 of his monthly mortgage payment is used to pay the lender's interest.

In addition to the principal amount borrowed, Bob would pay around $123,610 in interest over the course of a 30-year mortgage.

In conclusion, Bob gained knowledge about interest in real estate finance via this example, as well as how it affects his monthly mortgage payments and the overall amount of interest he would pay over the course of the loan. Bob and other borrowers may evaluate mortgage choices, determine if homeownership is affordable, and make well-informed finance decisions by having a solid understanding of how interest is calculated.

4. PITI

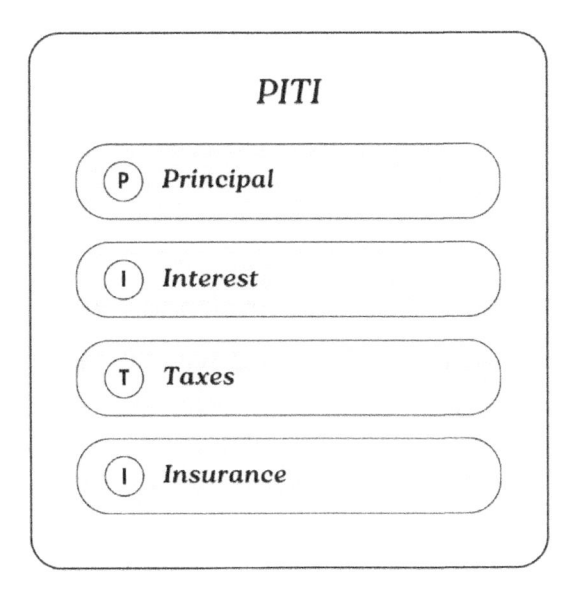

PITI
- **P** Principal
- **I** Interest
- **T** Taxes
- **I** Insurance

The acronym PITI, which stands for Principal, Interest, Taxes, and Insurance, denotes the four main expenses associated with a standard monthly mortgage payment. Since PITI includes all of the expenses related to house ownership, such as loan repayment, property taxes, and insurance premiums, it is crucial for both homeowners and prospective homebuyers to understand it. PITI is often used by lenders to determine a borrower's maximum loan amount that they are eligible for as well as to evaluate the borrower's capacity to finance a mortgage.

🔎 Practical Example in Real Estate

For instance: Situation

- Alice is thinking of spending $300,000 on a home, and she intends to get a mortgage to pay for it.
- She wants to compute her monthly mortgage payment and comprehend how PITI operates.

Goal:

- Recognize the meaning of PITI in financing for real estate.
- Determine Alice's monthly mortgage payment, accounting for insurance, taxes, principle, and interest.

PITI Estimate:

Calculate the Loan Amount:

Suppose Alice puts $60,000 down, or 20% of the $300,000 home, leaving her with a $240,000 mortgage debt.

Compute Interest and Principal Each Month:

- Alice's lender is willing to provide her a 30-year fixed-rate mortgage with an annual interest rate of 4.5%. The monthly principal and interest payment may be calculated by her using a mortgage calculator or an amortization plan.

- Alice uses a mortgage calculator to determine that, for a $240,000 loan with a 4.5% interest rate for 30 years, her monthly principal and interest payment would be around $1,216.04.

Monthly Property Tax Estimate:

- The location and assessed value of the property affect property taxes. By dividing the yearly property tax amount by twelve, Alice may calculate her expected monthly property taxes.

- Assuming Alice pays $3,000 in property taxes annually, her monthly payment would be $250.

Calculate Your Monthly Insurance Premiums:

- Homeowners insurance, which covers liability and property damage, is often needed. By dividing the yearly insurance premium by twelve, Alice may calculate her monthly insurance costs.

- Assuming Alice pays $1,200 in premiums for homeowners insurance year, her monthly insurance payment would be $100.

Determine PITI:

- The total of monthly property taxes, insurance premiums, and principal and interest payments is known as PITI.

- PITI is equal to $1,216.04 + $250 + $100 = $1,566.04 and is calculated as the monthly principal and interest payment plus monthly property taxes and insurance premiums.

Useful Illustration:

Alice pays around $1,566.04 in PITI each month towards her $240,000 home loan. This sum covers all of her monthly housing costs, including insurance premiums, property taxes, and loan payments.

In summary, Alice gained knowledge about PITI in real estate finance via this example, as well as how to figure out her monthly mortgage payment, which includes principle, interest, taxes, and insurance. Comprehending PITI helps Alice and other homeowners in setting aside funds for their housing costs and determining if homeownership is affordable. To assess a borrower's financial stability and establish whether they qualify for a home loan, lenders utilize PITI.

5. **Escrow Account**

An escrow account, often referred to as an impound account in real estate, is a bank account created by the lender to retain money for the borrower's use in paying costs associated with the property, such as homeowners insurance and property taxes. Together with the monthly mortgage payment, the lender also receives a percentage of these costs. The lender also oversees the distribution of cash when the bills are due. For borrowers, escrow accounts provide a practical means of planning ahead and guaranteeing prompt payment of costs associated with real estate.

🔍 Practical Example in Real Estate

For instance: Situation

- After deciding to open an escrow account with his lender, Bob chooses to get a mortgage to buy a $300,000 property.
- He wants to know how his monthly mortgage payments are affected by the escrow account and how it operates.

Goal:

- Recognize the meaning of an escrow account in the context of financing real estate.
- Determine Bob's monthly mortgage payment and the effect of his escrow payment.

Compute Escrow Account:

Calculate Property Taxes Each Year:

Bob pays $3,000 in property taxes annually.

Calculate Your Annual Premium for Homeowners Insurance:

The annual cost for Bob's homeowners insurance is $1,200.

Determine the Total Annual Escrow Costs:

Property taxes plus homeowners insurance premium equals total annual escrow expenses of $3,000 plus $1,200, or $4,200.

Calculate the Escrow Payment Each Month:

The monthly escrow payment is calculated by Bob's lender by dividing the total yearly escrow expenditures by 12.

Total Annual Escrow Expenses / 12 = $4,200 / 12 ≈ $350 is the monthly escrow payment.

Useful Illustration:

- Bob pays around $350 a month into escrow. His total monthly payment, or PITI (principal, interest, taxes, and insurance), is calculated by adding this sum to his principal and interest-only mortgage payment.

- For instance, Bob's total monthly mortgage payment (PITI) would be $1,550 ($1,200 P&I + $350 escrow) if his principal and interest payment (P&I) is $1,200 each month.

Bob gained knowledge about escrow accounts in real estate finance via this example, including how to handle and settle costs associated with real estate. Comprehending escrow accounts guarantees that homeowners insurance premiums and property taxes are paid on time, and it also helps borrowers like Bob plan their monthly mortgage payments. For certain mortgage products, lenders want escrow accounts in order to safeguard their interests and guarantee that the property is properly insured and lien-free.

5.2 Mortgage

A mortgage is a kind of loan that is taken out to fund the purchase of real estate, usually a house or other property, from a lender or financial organization. The lender lends cash to the borrower, who then repays the funds over time with interest. The borrower, a purchaser, offers the property as collateral for the loan. One of the most popular ways to finance real estate purchases is via a mortgage, which enables people to acquire properties without having to pay the whole amount up front.

🔍 Practical Example in Real Estate

- Alice does not have enough funds to cover the whole upfront cost of the $250,000 home she wants to buy.

- She chooses to finance the purchase with a mortgage and is curious about how it works.

Goal:

- Recognize the meaning of a mortgage in relation to finance for real estate.
- Determine Alice's monthly mortgage payment and the total amount she will pay in interest over the course of the loan.

Calculate a Mortgage:

Calculate the Loan Amount:

Assuming Alice puts $50,000 down as 20% of the $250,000 house's total cost, her mortgage loan balance will be $200,000.

Choose the Interest Rate and Mortgage Term:

Alice decides on a 4.5% interest rate, 30-year fixed-rate mortgage.

Compute Interest and Principal Each Month:

Alice determines her monthly principal and interest payment for the $200,000 mortgage loan at a 4.5% interest rate for 30 years by using a mortgage calculator or calculation.

PMT(Interest Rate, Number of Payments, Loan Amount) = PMT(4.5%, 30 Years * 12 Months/Year, $200,000) ≈ $1,013.37 is the monthly principal and interest payment.

Alice pays around $1,013.37 in principle and interest each month on her $200,000 home loan. This sum is the percentage of her monthly payment that is used to settle the loan debt and cover the lender's interest.

In addition to the principal amount borrowed, Alice would pay around $164,813.20 in interest over the course of a 30-year mortgage.

Alice gained knowledge about mortgages in real estate financing via this example, including how they function to fund house purchases. Comprehending mortgages helps homebuyers such as Alice in evaluating their financing alternatives, planning their monthly expenses, and arriving at well-informed selections about homeownership. Lenders provide borrowers with a range of mortgage options with varying periods and interest rates, so they may choose the one that best fits their needs in terms of both long-term objectives and finances.

1. **Definition and Introduction**

"Definition and Introduction" in the context of real estate refers to the preliminary phase of comprehending fundamental ideas and ideas associated with the sector. This phase usually entails being acquainted with the basic terminologies, ideas, and procedures related to investments, property ownership, and real estate transactions.

🔍 Practical Example in Real Estate

For illustration, consider the following scenario: John, a recent college graduate, wants to work in the real estate sector. Although he is unfamiliar with the terms and ideas used in the real estate industry, he has heard of a number of chances in the sector. John makes the decision to begin by being familiar with the fundamental terminologies and overviews of real estate.

Goal:

- Recognize the basic words and ideas in real estate.
- Learn the fundamentals of how the real estate market works.

Definition and Summary:

Property:

Land, structures, and natural resources like minerals and bodies of water that are affixed to the land are all considered real estate. Residential, business, industrial, and agricultural assets are all included.

Ownership of Property:

Real estate ownership gives people or organizations the legal ability to hold, use, and dispose of it. Leasehold, easements, or fee simple absolute are the three types of ownership.

Transactions in Real Estate:

Purchasing, selling, or leasing real estate are all considered forms of real estate transactions. Usually, in order to transfer ownership rights, they need agreements, court papers, and contracts.

Realtors:

Licenced professionals known as real estate agents help customers purchase, sell, or rent real estate. They assist in facilitating transactions by serving as middlemen between buyers and sellers.

Examination of the Market:

Analyzing the dynamics of supply and demand, market trends, and economic variables that influence real estate prices in a certain location or market segment are all part of market analysis.

Properties for Investment:

Real estate assets bought with the goal of earning income or appreciating in value are known as investment properties. Land held for development, commercial structures, and rental assets are among them.

Funding:

The term "financing" describes the sources and techniques used to raise money for real estate deals, including loans, mortgages, and other forms of alternative financing.

Useful Illustration:

John studies these basic phrases and ideas as part of his real estate education. He attends seminars, reads books, and enrolls in online courses to further his knowledge of the real estate sector. He gains knowledge about the functions of real estate brokers, the ownership of real estate, and the many kinds of real estate transactions.

John begins his real estate career in this example by being acquainted with the fundamental terminologies and overviews of the field. Gaining an understanding of these core ideas sets the stage for more research and education in the real estate industry.

2. Calculation of Mortgage

Finding the monthly payment necessary to repay a loan used to fund the acquisition of real estate over a certain term—typically with interest—is the first step in calculating a mortgage. The loan amount, interest rate, and loan period are all taken into consideration in the computation. To precisely calculate mortgage payments, a number of mathematical formulae and internet calculators are available.

🔍 Practical Example in Real Estate

For illustration purposes, let's say Alice wants to buy a home for $300,000 and plans to get a mortgage to pay for it. She wants to know how much her mortgage will cost each month.

Goal:

Recognize how to use mathematical methods to determine a mortgage payment.

Calculate the Loan Amount:

Assume Alice puts 20% of the $300,000 home down, leaving her with a $240,000 mortgage loan balance.

Choose the Interest Rate and Mortgage Term:

Alice decides on a 4.5% interest rate, 30-year fixed-rate mortgage.

Utilize the Mortgage Payment Formula:

The present value of an annuity formula serves as the basis for the mortgage payment calculation formula. The equation is:

$$M = P \times \frac{r(1+r)^n}{(1+r)^n - 1}$$

where:
- M = monthly mortgage payment
- P = principal loan amount
- r = monthly interest rate (annual interest rate divided by 12)
- n = number of payments (loan term in years multiplied by 12)

4. **Calculate Monthly Mortgage Payment:**
   - For Alice's mortgage:
     - Principal loan amount (P) = $240,000
     - Annual interest rate (r) = 4.5%
     - Monthly interest rate (r) = 4.5% / 12 = 0.375%
     - Loan term (n) = 30 years * 12 months/year = 360 months

   Substituting the values into the formula:

   $$M = 240000 \times \frac{0.00375(1+0.00375)^{360}}{(1+0.00375)^{360} - 1}$$

   $$M \approx 1216.04$$

Useful Illustration:

With a 4.5% interest rate and a $240,000 mortgage loan over 30 years, Alice will pay around $1,216.04 per month for her mortgage. Her whole monthly payment, principle and interest included, is represented by this sum.

Alice gained knowledge on how to use mathematical formulae to determine her monthly mortgage payment from this example. Comprehending the methodology behind the mortgage computation enables borrowers such as Alice to effectively manage their monthly spending and make well-informed choices about homeownership. Additionally, there are online mortgage calculators that make computations easier and provide instantaneous monthly payment projections.

3. **Conventional Loan Down Payments and Calculations**

A conventional loan is a kind of home loan for which the government does not provide insurance or guarantees. A down payment is the first payment made by the borrower towards the purchase price of the property, and it is usually required for conventional loans. The down payment amount is based on a number of variables, including the borrower's creditworthiness, the loan programme, and the lender's criteria. It is indicated as a percentage of the purchase price of the property.

🔍 Practical Example in Real Estate

Let's examine traditional loan down payments and computations using the following real-world example:

For illustration purposes, let's say Alice wants to buy a home for $300,000 and is applying for a traditional mortgage. She's curious about the down payment criteria and how much one must put down.

Goal:

Recognize the formula used to determine down payments for conventional loans.

Calculating the Down Payment for a Conventional Loan:

Calculate the percentage of the down payment:

- A minimum down payment of 5% to 20% of the purchase price is a typical requirement for conventional loans, however specific requirements may differ.
- Assume Alice has enough cash on hand to cover a 20% down payment.

Find the Amount of the Down Payment:

- Multiply the purchase price of the property by the down payment percentage to get the down payment amount.
- Purchase Price × Down Payment Percentage = $300,000 × 20% = $60,000 is the down payment amount.

Useful Illustration:

With a traditional loan, Alice will pay $60,000 down, or 20% of the $300,000 purchase price, for her new home. This implies that Alice will make a down payment of $60,000 and that the mortgage loan will fund the remaining $240,000.

Alice gained knowledge about conventional loan down payments and their computations from this case. For borrowers like Alice, knowing down payment requirements is crucial to figuring out how much money they need to save up front and determining if they qualify for a mortgage loan. Greater down payments may also translate into cheaper monthly mortgage payments and lower interest expenses over the course of the loan.

4. **Mortgage Amortization**

The practice of gradually repaying a mortgage debt via consistent principle and interest payments is known as mortgage amortization. A part of each mortgage payment is used to pay down the principal (loan amount), while the remaining amount is used to pay interest. The sum lowers during the loan period until the loan is paid off in full.

🔍 **Practical Example in Real Estate**

Example:

Suppose Alice wants to buy a house for $200,000. She gets a 30-year fixed-rate mortgage. The yearly interest rate on the mortgage is 4.5%.

Goal:

Comprehend the principles and interest payments throughout time, as well as the monthly mortgage payment and how mortgage amortization works.

Calculate Amortization of Mortgage:

Determine Your Monthly Mortgage Payment:

We use the present value of an annuity calculation to get the monthly mortgage payment:

$$M = P \times \frac{r(1+r)^n}{(1+r)^n - 1}$$

where:

- M = monthly mortgage payment
- P = principal loan amount ($200,000)
- r = monthly interest rate (annual interest rate divided by 12)
- n = number of payments (loan term in years multiplied by 12)

- Given that the loan term is 30 years, or 360 months, and the annual interest rate is 4.5%, the monthly interest rate (r) is $\frac{4.5}{12}$ or 0.375%.
- Substituting the values into the formula:

$$M = 200,000 \times \frac{0.00375(1+0.00375)^{360}}{(1+0.00375)^{360} - 1}$$

$$M \approx 1,013.37$$

- Alice's monthly mortgage payment is approximately $1,013.37.

Determine the Amortization Plan:

An amortization schedule breaks out each mortgage payment into its component parts, indicating how much goes towards principal and interest for each time period.

Alice may create an amortization schedule that displays the monthly payments, remaining loan amount, and interest paid for each term using a spreadsheet or online calculator.

Useful Illustration:

Regarding Alice's mortgage:

- $1,013.37 is the monthly mortgage payment.
- About $164,813.20 in interest was paid overall during a 30-year period.
- The majority of Alice's first payment goes towards interest; the principal amount is paid in lesser amounts. But as long as she keeps up her payments, the amount allotted to principal rises and the amount allotted to interest falls.

This example covered mortgage amortization, which is the process of progressively repaying a mortgage debt by making consistent principle and interest-only payments.

Comprehending mortgage amortization facilitates monthly payment planning and helps borrowers like Alice see how their loan amount reduces over time. Furthermore, examining an amortization plan might provide information about the overall amount of interest paid as well as the effects of increasing payments or refinancing the loan.

Chapter 6:
Closing Statements

A closing statement, often referred to as a settlement statement or HUD-1 form, is a document created by the closing agent in real estate transactions that lists all the financial information pertaining to the sale or acquisition of a property. The buyer and seller's financial transactions and out-of-pocket costs throughout the closing process are summarized in the closing statement.

🔎 Practical Example in Real Estate

For illustration, let's say Alice is paying $250,000 to Bob for a home. The closing agent has completed the closing statement, which includes all of the transaction's financial information, and the closing date is getting closer.

Goal:

Recognize the elements of a closing statement and how they are determined.

Components of the Closing Statement:

Purchase Cost:

The agreed upon sum that Alice, the buyer, will pay Bob, the seller, for the property is known as the buying price. The purchasing price in this instance is $250,000.

Divided Costs:

Costs known as prorated expenditures are split between the buyer and the seller according to the percentage of the ownership term that falls within each party's purview.

Property taxes, homeowners association (HOA) dues, and utility costs are examples of common prorated expenditures.

Closing Expenses:

Fees related to the real estate transaction's closure, including attorney fees, title insurance, appraisal fees, and loan origination fees, are referred to as closing expenses. Usually, both the buyer and the seller are responsible for covering these expenses, however the exact split may change based on regional laws and discussions.

Adjustments & Credits:

Any payments or reimbursements made to either party at closure are represented by credits and adjustments. Earnest money deposits, seller concessions, or credits for improvements or repairs are a few examples.

Insurance and Taxes:

The closing statement may also contain payments for insurance and taxes. This covers prepaid or collected property taxes and homeowners insurance premiums at closing in order to create escrow accounts.

Useful Illustration:

The principal transaction value of $250,000 is indicated in Alice and Bob's closing statement. Prorated property taxes, closing expenses, and adjustments are also itemized to illustrate how Alice and Bob's combined debt is determined.

Closing statements, which provide a thorough analysis of the financial aspects of the sale or purchase of a property, are crucial records in real estate transactions. Comprehending the constituents of a closing statement guarantees openness and precision in the closing procedure and aids buyers and sellers in appreciating the financial consequences of the deal.

6.1 Escrow or Closing; Tax Aspects of Transferring Title to Real Property

The transfer of title to real property in real estate transactions entails a number of tax considerations that must be made during the escrow or closing procedure. Property taxes, transfer taxes, and possible tax ramifications for both the seller and the buyer are some of these tax-related factors. It is essential for both parties to comprehend these tax-related factors in order to guarantee adherence to tax regulations and reduce monetary obligations.

🔎 Practical Example in Real Estate

For instance:

In this scenario, Alice is paying $300,000 to Bob for a property. They have to think about the tax ramifications of changing the property's title as they get ready for the closing procedure.

Goal:

Gain an understanding of the tax implications of transferring ownership of real estate during escrow or closing.

Tax Implications of Real Property Title Transfers:

Property-related taxes:

- Local governments impose property taxes according to the property's assessed value. Property taxes are normally prorated between the buyer and the seller during the closing process according to the percentage of the property tax year that each will hold the property.

- For instance, if the property tax year starts on January 1st and ends on July 1st, Alice will be in charge of property taxes starting on July 1st and Bob will be in charge from January 1st to June 30th.

MASTERING REAL ESTATE MATH FOR SUCCESS

Transfer Taxes:

State or municipal governments apply transfer taxes, also referred to as conveyance taxes or deed transfer taxes, on the transfer of real property from one party to another. Depending on local laws, these taxes are normally computed using the property's selling price and paid by the seller, the buyer, or both parties.

In this instance, depending on the jurisdiction and the conditions established in the purchase agreement, Bob or Alice may be responsible for paying transfer taxes.

Tax Repercussions for the Purchaser:

Alice may be qualified for some homeownership-related tax advantages as the buyer, including deductions for property taxes, mortgage interest, and points paid on the loan. Alice's taxable income and total tax obligation may be decreased with the use of these tax advantages.

Effects of Taxation on the Seller:

Bob would have to pay capital gains tax as the seller on any proceeds from the sale of the property. But Bob could qualify for other exclusions or deductions. For example, the main residence exclusion lets people deduct a percentage of their capital gains from taxes if the property has been used as their principal home for a certain amount of time.

Useful Illustration:

To make sure that all tax ramifications of transferring title to the property are taken care of, Alice and Bob will collaborate with their respective real estate agents, lawyers, or escrow officers throughout the closing process. This entails figuring out transfer tax liabilities, computing prorated property taxes, and comprehending any possible tax ramifications for both parties.

This example examined the tax implications of transferring ownership of real estate during an escrow or closing. Comprehending these tax implications is crucial for both purchasers and vendors to guarantee adherence to regulatory frameworks, reduce monetary obligations, and capitalize on any potential tax advantages linked to homeownership.

1. Proration of Taxes

In real estate, proration of taxes refers to the process of dividing the buyer's and seller's property tax obligations according to the percentage of the tax year that each party holds the property. Local governments often assess property taxes once a year, and the property owner is responsible for paying them. To guarantee that all parties pay their fair share of taxes for the time they possess the property, property taxes are prorated between the buyer and the seller during a real estate transaction.

🔎 Practical Example in Real Estate

For instance, in this scenario, Alice is paying $300,000 to Bob for a property. The residence has an October 1st closing date and $3,600 in yearly property taxes. For the current tax year, they must determine the prorated property taxes.

Goal: Gain knowledge on how to divide property taxes in a real estate transaction between the seller and the buyer.

Proration of Taxes Determined:

Calculate the Annual Total Property Taxes:

The house's total yearly property taxes come to $3,600.

Determine the Rate of Daily Property Tax:

- Divide the total yearly property taxes by the number of days in the tax year to get the daily property tax rate.

- With October 1st as the ending date, the tax year has 92 days left in it (365 days minus 273 days already passed).

- Total Annual Property Taxes / Number of Days in Tax Year = $3,600 / 365 = $9.86 per day is the daily property tax rate.

Compute the Property Taxes Due on Seller's Portion:

- Property taxes are Bob's responsibility as the seller up to the closing date, which is October 1.

- The seller has owned the property for 273 days, starting on January 1st and ending on September 30th.

- Seller's Share of Property Taxes = Daily Rate of Property Tax × Total Days of Property Ownership = $9.86 × 273 ≈ $2,691.78

Determine the Buyer's Share of Property Taxes:

- Property taxes are Alice's (the buyer's) responsibility starting on October 1st, the closing date.

- The buyer will own the property for 92 days, starting on October 1 and ending on December 31.

- Property taxes paid by the buyer are calculated as follows: Daily Property Tax Rate × Total Days of Property Ownership = $9.86 × 92 ≈ $907.12.

Useful Illustration:

In this scenario, Bob would owe Alice around $2,691.78 for property taxes paid between January 1st and September 30th, when he held the property, and Alice would owe $907.12 for property taxes paid between October 1st and December 31st, when she owned the property.

In conclusion, tax proration makes sure that each party pays their fair share of property taxes according to the percentage of the tax year that they each hold the property. In order to guarantee a just and equal allocation of tax obligations, it is crucial for both purchasers and sellers to understand how to prorate property taxes during real estate transactions.

2. **Proration of Rent**

When a property is sold or transferred in the middle of the rental term, the process of splitting the rental payment between the buyer and the seller is known as proration of rent in real estate. By doing this, it is made sure that everyone pays their fair share of the rent according to the amount of time they spend using the property. In real estate transactions involving rental properties, such apartment complexes or single-family houses with tenants already living there, proportion of rent is often used.

🔍 Practical Example in Real Estate

For instance, in this scenario, Alice is paying Bob $400,000. She is buying a rental property. The rental income from the property is $2,000 per month, and October 15th is the closing date. The prorated rent for the current month must be determined.

Goal:

Acquire knowledge on how to divide rent in a real estate transaction including rental units between the buyer and the seller.

Rent Proration Calculation:

Calculate the Total Monthly Rent:

The property is rented out for a total of $2,000.

Determine the Daily Rental Rate:

- Divide the total monthly rent by the number of days in the month to get the daily rent cost.

- There are 17 days left in the month of October (October has 31 days) since October 15th is the closure date.

- Total Monthly Rent / Number of Days in a Month = $2,000 / 31 = $64.52 per day is the daily rent rate.

Compute the Seller's Share of the Rent:

- For the part of the month that he holds the property (October 1st to October 15th), Bob, the seller, is entitled to rent.
- The seller has owned the property for 15 days.
- Seller's Share of Rent is equal to the Daily Rent Rate times the Total Days Seller Owns Property, which comes to $64.52 × 15 ≈ $967.80.

Determine the Buyer's Rent Share:

- For the part of October that she owns the home (October 16 to October 31), Alice, the buyer, is entitled to rent.
- The buyer has owned the property for 16 days.
- Buyer's Share of Rent is equal to Daily Rent Rate × Days of Property Ownership, or $64.52 × 16 ≈ $1,032.32.

Useful Illustration:

In this scenario, Alice would get the remaining $1,032.32 for the rent received during her ownership of the property (October 16 to October 31), while Bob would owe her around $967.80 for the rent earned during his ownership (October 1 to October 15).

Rent proration guarantees that each party receives an equitable percentage of rental revenue proportional to the duration of each party's ownership of the property. In real estate transactions involving rental properties, it is crucial for both buyers and sellers to understand how to prorate rent in order to facilitate a seamless transfer of rental revenue between parties.

3. Proration of Homeowner's Fees

When a property is sold or transferred in the middle of the rental term, the process of splitting the rental payment between the buyer and the seller is known as proration of rent in real estate. By doing this, it is made sure that everyone pays their fair share of the rent according to the amount of time they spend using the property. In real estate transactions involving rental properties, such apartment complexes or single-family houses with tenants already living there, proportion of rent is often used.

🔍 Practical Example in Real Estate

For instance, in this scenario, Alice is paying Bob $400,000. She is buying a rental property. The rental income from the property is $2,000 per month, and October 15th is the closing date. The prorated rent for the current month must be determined.

Goal:

Acquire knowledge on how to divide rent in a real estate transaction including rental units between the buyer and the seller.

Rent Proration Calculation:

Calculate the Total Monthly Rent:

The property is rented out for a total of $2,000.

Determine the Daily Rental Rate:

- Divide the total monthly rent by the number of days in the month to get the daily rent cost.
- There are 17 days left in the month of October (October has 31 days) since October 15th is the closure date.
- Total Monthly Rent / Number of Days in a Month = $2,000 / 31 = $64.52 per day is the daily rent rate.

Compute the Seller's Share of the Rent:

- For the part of the month that he holds the property (October 1st to October 15th), Bob, the seller, is entitled to rent.
- The seller has owned the property for 15 days.

- Seller's Share of Rent is equal to the Daily Rent Rate times the Total Days Seller Owns Property, which comes to $64.52 × 15 ≈ $967.80.

Determine the Buyer's Rent Share:

- For the part of October that she owns the home (October 16 to October 31), Alice, the buyer, is entitled to rent.

- The buyer has owned the property for 16 days.

- Buyer's Share of Rent is equal to Daily Rent Rate × Days of Property Ownership, or $64.52 × 16 ≈ $1,032.32.

Useful Illustration:

In this scenario, Alice would get the remaining $1,032.32 for the rent received during her ownership of the property (October 16 to October 31), while Bob would owe her around $967.80 for the rent earned during his ownership (October 1 to October 15).

Rent proration guarantees that each party receives an equitable percentage of rental revenue proportional to the duration of each party's ownership of the property. In real estate transactions involving rental properties, it is crucial for both buyers and sellers to understand how to prorate rent in order to facilitate a seamless transfer of rental revenue between parties.

4. **Proration of Mortgage Payments**

When a property is transferred or sold in the middle of a mortgage payment cycle, the procedure known as proration of mortgage payments in real estate is used. The buyer and seller split the mortgage payment equally. Principal, interest, taxes, and insurance are usually covered by mortgage payments (PITI). By using proration, each party pays their fair share of the mortgage according to the percentage of time they have owned the property.

🔍 Practical Example in Real Estate

For instance, in this scenario, Alice is paying $300,000 to Bob for a property. The home has a $1,500 monthly mortgage payment that covers principle, interest, taxes, and insurance (PITI). May 15th is the last day to submit. The prorated mortgage payment for the current month must be determined.

Goal: Recognize how to divide mortgage payments in a real estate transaction between the buyer and the seller.

Calculating the Proration of Mortgage Payments:

Calculate Your Entire Monthly Mortgage Payment:

The home has a $1,500 monthly mortgage payment.

Determine the Daily Rate of Mortgage Payment:

- Divide the total monthly payment by the number of days in the month to get the daily mortgage payment rate.

- There are 16 days left in May (assuming a 31-day month) since May 15th is the closure date.

- Total Monthly Mortgage Payment / Number of Days in a Month = $1,500 / 31 = $48.39 per day is the daily mortgage payment rate.

Determine the Seller's Share of the Mortgage Payment:

- For the part of the month that he owns the home (May 1st to May 15th), Bob, the seller, is in charge of making the mortgage payments.

- The seller has owned the property for 15 days.

- Seller's Share of the Mortgage Payment = Rate of Daily Mortgage Payment × Total Days of Property Ownership = $48.39 × 15 ≈ $725.85

Determine the Buyer's Share of the Mortgage Payment:

- For the period that Alice, the buyer, holds the home (May 16 to May 31), she is liable for the mortgage payments.
- The buyer has owned the property for 16 days.
- Purchaser's Share of Mortgage Payment = Rate of Daily Mortgage Payment × Number of Days of Property Ownership = $48.39 × 16 ≈ $774.24

Useful Illustration:

In this scenario, Bob would owe Alice around $725.85 for the mortgage payments made between May 1 and May 15 while he was the property's owner, and Alice would be in charge of paying the remaining $774.24 for the mortgage payments made between May 16 and May 31.

The practice of prorating mortgage payments guarantees that each party pays a reasonable fraction of the mortgage costs in accordance with the length of time they have owned the property. In order to guarantee a fair division of financial obligations, it is crucial for both buyers and sellers in real estate transactions to understand how to prorate mortgage payments.

5. Proration of Insurances

When a property is sold or transferred in the middle of the insurance term, the process of splitting the insurance premiums between the buyer and the seller is known as proration of insurances in real estate. This guarantees that, according to the duration of their ownership of the property, each party pays their appropriate share of the insurance premiums. Homeowners, flood, and mortgage insurance are among the insurances that are often prorated.

🔍 Practical Example in Real Estate

For illustration, let's say Alice is paying $250,000 to Bob for a home. The property has an annual homeowners insurance cost of $1,200, and the insurance policy is in effect from

January 1 to December 31. The 15th of July is the deadline. For the months that remain in the policy term, they must compute the prorated homeowners insurance premium.

Goal:

Gain knowledge on how to divide insurance costs between the seller and the buyer in a real estate transaction.

Calculating the Proration of Insurances:

Calculate the Total Annual Insurance Premium:

The property has a $1,200 yearly total homeowners insurance premium.

Compute Monthly Premium for Insurance:

- Divide the whole yearly payment by 12 months to get the monthly insurance premium.
- Total Annual Insurance Premium / 12 = $1,200 / 12 = $100 monthly is the monthly insurance premium.

Determine the Daily Premium Rate for Insurance:

- Divide the monthly insurance payment by the total number of days in the month to get the daily premium rate.
- Assuming a non-leap year, there are 169 days left in the year because the closure date is July 15th.
- Daily Insurance Premium Rate: $100 / 365 ≈ $0.27 each day; Monthly Insurance Premium / Number of Days in Month

Determine the Seller's Share of the Insurance Premium:

- For the month of January through July 15 of each year that he owns the property, Bob, the seller, is in charge of paying the insurance rates.

- 195 days are the number of days the seller owns the property (January 1st to July 15th)

- Seller's Share of Insurance Premium = Rate of Daily Insurance Premium × Days of Property Ownership = $0.27 × 195 ≈ $52.65.

Determine the Buyer's Share of the Insurance Premium:

- During the period from July 16 to December 31 of the year that she owns the property, Alice, the buyer, is in charge of paying the insurance premiums.

- 171 days are the number of days the buyer owns the property (from July 16 to December 31).

- The insurance premium rate divided by the number of days the buyer owns the property yields the buyer's portion, which comes out to $0.27 × 171 = $46.17.

In this scenario, Bob would owe Alice around $52.65 for insurance premiums paid between January 1st and July 15th, when he owned the property, and Alice would be liable for the remaining $46.17 for insurance premiums paid between July 16th and December 31st, when she owned the property.

Proration of insurance guarantees that, according to the length of time each party has owned the property, each party pays their appropriate share of the insurance premiums. In order to guarantee a fair division of financial obligations, it is crucial for both buyers and sellers in real estate transactions to understand how to prorate insurance rates.

Conclusion

In summary, "Mastering Real Estate Math for Success" gives you the fundamental understanding and abilities needed to successfully negotiate the intricate world of real estate transactions. This comprehensive book provides a strong foundation for success in the real estate sector, from learning fundamental mathematical concepts to diving into complex calculations for transactions, land measurement, valuation, market analysis, financing, and closing statements.

You have gained an understanding of the nuances of proration, commission structures, and taxes in real estate transactions, as well as how to use fractions, percentages, decimals, and equations efficiently throughout the text. They now have a better understanding of the several land measuring systems and valuation techniques that are necessary to determine the exact value of a property. Furthermore, the book offers a comprehension of financing alternatives and the nuances of closing statements, guaranteeing that you are adequately equipped to maneuver through each phase of a real estate transaction with assurance and expertise.

The book equips you with the information and resources you need to make wise choices and carry out transactions precisely. It is a priceless tool for novice and experienced real estate professionals alike, as well as anyone hoping to succeed in the fast-paced real estate industry. By the time you complete the last chapter, readers will have the knowledge and self-assurance to take on real estate obstacles head-on, laying the groundwork for a fruitful and rewarding career in the exciting field of real estate.

Made in the USA
Las Vegas, NV
18 March 2025